FREE BO1

There is hope... Regain

MW00984880

https://jimlange.net/bonus

A **FREE** Membership Website for Men
to Radically Grow Yourself and Revolutionize Your Marriage.

You'd be shocked at how many husbands have experienced disrespect, manipulation, and rejection in their marriages. Difficulties with your wife can leave you feeling like a failure, hopeless, and worn out.

I know; I've been there. God wants peace and rest in your home.

LEARN TO NAVIGATE
Navigate relationships with people who
control, manipulate, and reject you.

REGAIN HOPE.
Get unstuck and experience hope again.

RECONNECT.
Reconnect to your spouse emotionally,
relationally, and sexually.

You don't have to be stuck in a painful marriage for the rest of your life. Get access to your FREE Resources on the *Happy Wife Happy Life Deception* Bonus Site!

Get your free resources here...

https://jimlange.net/bonus

THE HAPPY WIFE HAPPY LIFE DECEPTION

HOW TO STOP WALKING ON EGGSHELLS & BE THE MAN YOU WERE MADE TO BE

JIM LANGE

Published by

FIVEFEET
TWENTY
LIFE LESSONS FROM ABOVE

Published by Five Feet Twenty

ISBN 978-0-9886137-7-5

Cover design: Jennifer Lassiter

Editor: Ben Wolf (www.benwolf.com/editing-services)

The names and some of the details in the stories in this book have been changed for confidentiality reasons.

TABLE OF CONTENTS

Modern man is marked by timidity and passivity. The effects are toxic, especially to marriages. Jim Lange shows us the way through, with counsel that will surprise you, as it did me.

This book is bold, but we're ripe for straight talk on the topic of producing healthy marriages, for they are the hinge-point to the survival of our social order.

~John D. Beckett
Chairman, The Beckett Companies
Author, *Loving Monday* and *Mastering Monday*

"When God created us in His image, He created us male and female. I believe this reveals that the fullest, most complete, and most powerful representation of God in the earth is when men and women co-labor together in the love, honor, respect and unity of God's character and nature.

Nowhere is this more evident than in marriage. Strong, healthy, loving, respectful, honoring marriages empower husbands, wives, families, societies and nations. No wonder the devil works so hard to sow division and discord into these divine unions.

If you are a husband whose marriage is under attack, there is wisdom and hope in the pages of Jim Lange's book. Dig in and discover the transformative power of walking in the fullness of love, honor and respect as the husbands we are called to be. For ourselves. For our wonderful wives. And for our families, nations and the world."

~Robert Hotchkin
Men on the Frontlines
MenontheFrontlines.com

A dangerous and unexpected cocktail is created when a passive man and an abusive woman come together. Men allow women to neglect, emotionally abuse and hamster-wheel them into a spiral of conflict and self-hatred.

Fights over attention and money are barbed with accusations. Sex is grudging and infrequent. Wives, counselors, culture and namby-pamby preachers dispense lame advice. (Hint: Flowers and chocolates will <u>never</u> dig you out.)

Here, Jim Lange gets naked about his own failures and points today's castrated Christian man to a superior way.

~Perry Marshall
Author, *Ultimate Guide to Google Advertising,*
80/20 Sales & Marketing, and Evolution 2.0

As a person who studies and researches human behavior for living, I want to thank Jim for providing all of us with great case studies, lessons, counsel, and coaching about how to take on, and defeat some of the critically important challenges associated with relationship dynamics in the 21st century.

His book provides readers with an emotional and relationship-oriented "toolkit" that each of us can use to look in the mirror to see if we are living up to our relationship responsibilities in a fashion that allows our faith to make an impact our lives and interactions with others!

Jim has taken on a very sensitive topic head-on and has used Scripture in a way that is essential to realize our full potential, and to better share our lives with others! Thanks Jim!

~Clinton O. Longenecker, PhD.
Distinguished Professor of Leadership and Organizational
Excellence, Executive Coach, Consultant, Speaker,
and Best-Selling Author

Thank you, Jim, for having the courage to write this book. This teaching can apply to any relationship where passivity allows one person in a relationship to control the other.

Thank you for sharing how this controlling behavior can be done from wives toward husbands when we live in a world that mainly only speaks of husbands hurting wives.I recommend this book to anyone who may be in a controlling relationship that is holding them back from all God has for them.

If we ever do fully understand how much God loves us, so we can love ourselves in that way, and with that understanding, then loving our spouses and others will not be such a difficult task. God bless you and protect you as you move forward with His truth.

~Ford Taylor
Founder FSH Consulting Group/TL-Transformational Leadership

In The Happy Wife, Happy Life Deception, *Jim has touched on a topic that is of vital importance in the body of Christ: the knowledge of God and how important it is to have and understand it.*

This book reveals the truth of what happens in a marriage, or any relationship, when we don't clearly see who God is. Jim also shows us how the fear of man and people-pleasing can wreak havoc on relationships and marriages.

Thank you, Jim, for exposing the lies many of us believe and pointing people to Jesus. What we understand about God affects everything in our lives—and especially in our relationships! I recommend this book not only for men but for women as well!"

~Michelle Seidler
Prophetic Advisor, Executive Coach, Speaker, Equipper
Michelle Seidler Ministries

During 45 years of counseling and mentoring, I have watched the viral influence of culture—and its nature in the emasculation of boys, men, fathers and husbands—infiltrate our relationships.

My well-meaning mental health peers, both in and out of the Church, are pulled into this shipwreck of lies because there is no other voice to express the collateral damages of unbalanced roles.

Jim speaks into this deception, cuts across the #trending fad of our rationalized current world opinion, and calls us back to balance. He speaks both from personal experience and with a burdened passion to help as many as possible leave this 21st century Titanic.

His is a challenging voice, calling us to see the truth of our wonderful male and female differences. He calls us back to the balanced freedom Jesus gave us when He said, "you shall know the truth, and the truth shall set you free."

~Dr. James G Johnson, PhD, DCC
Lead Christian Counselor/Executive Director:
Keys4-L.I.F.E. Ministry
Best-selling author, *Grace: Orphans No More* and *Marriage Made Simple*

———

In The Happy Wife, Happy Life Deception, *Jim Lange challenges men to walk in the role of empowered leadership in one of life's challenging relationships: marriage.*

He gives practical steps of surrender, growth, and freedom in being the husband God calls men to be. Start the journey from passivity to Biblical masculinity today!

~Pastor Chris Bonham
Grace Family Church
Tampa, FL

In my work with leaders, I often advise couples. One thing I see repeatedly is an unhealthy dynamic at play in their marriages in which one spouse is dominant and the other timid.

In this book, Jim has cut to the heart of the matter. The real-life stories he shares are a snapshot of what Christian marriages look like in America today. We have a problem, and this book offers a solution. Brothers and sisters, read this book as a student seeking truth, breakthrough, and freedom.

~Melvin Pillay
Speaker & Advisor
The Prophetic Whiteboard

***

Years ago, I asked a young man why he wanted to be mentored. He responded, "I want to learn from your mistakes." In his book, The Happy Wife, Happy Life Deception, *Jim Lange not only presents the positive, biblically based principles he has discovered through 30 years of experience in marriage, but also invites the reader to learn from his mistakes and failures.*

Marriage is under attack in the 21st century, and husbands are the primary target. In his engaging style, Jim offers honest, transparent insights into how men today can survive and thrive in what's become a marital minefield. In his book you'll find much wisdom in how we can become the godly husbands and spiritual leaders God has called each of us to be.

~Robert J. Tamasy
Author, *Business at Its Best*
and *The Heart of Mentoring*

In a fallen world, all of us in marriage wrestle with the challenges of nurturing the most significant, intimate human relationship we have in our lives—the relationship we have with our spouse.

Much has been written about how "we" can be a better couple, or how "you" can better understand "me," but how do we stay true to ourselves as men in the midst of marital pressure? How do we honor our spouse while also holding fast to the truth that God has for us?

These are challenging questions, and Jim Lange has created a crucial conversation around this. I recommend his book not just to those struggling in a marriage but to all of us seeking to grow in our marriages.

~**Chuck Proudfit**
Founder & President
At Work On Purpose

Jim offers a fresh perspective on love, marriage, and relationships. He skillfully deconstructs many assumptions and misreadings of the Bible which have bred great dysfunction and damage.

I'm grateful for his wisdom and can personally attest to his character and integrity. Countless lives will be positively impacted by this important work.

~**Dr. Kirk Schneemann**
Lead Pastor, First Alliance Church, Toledo, OH

I have followed Jim Lange for a number of years and enjoyed his insights into living as a Christian man in our world. Before I read this book, I knew of Christian husbands who had some issues in their relationship with their wives, but I could not identify what was happening.

Jim presents an excellent analysis of the issues which I suspect are *unclear and yet common to many. By using case studies, he makes the material interesting and easy to understand.*

I also like that he is not pushing a formula for handling things but instead shares practical ways to apply Biblical and spiritual precepts and principles to allow for the Lord's direction in individual situations.

I highly recommend reading this book because, even if you do not have this problem in your marriage, I'm confident you will know several men who need to deal with it.

The marriage relationship has been under lots of pressure recently, and Jim has hit the nail on the head in identifying what is wrong and how to find a solution.

~W. Charles Hollensed, D. C.
Past President
Christian Chiropractors Association

The Happy Wife, Happy Life Deception *is an openly candid journey of men who have felt like failures in their marriages.*

By challenging lies and uncovering true identity—God's design for identity—men find freedom to be who God has called them to be. Thanks, Jim, for writing this book and giving men permission and a voice to join you in authentic manhood.

~Cheryl Kinnersley, PCC, BCPCC
Northwest Ohio Christian Counseling, Ltd.

A great marriage requires work and two people who are intentional about their commitment to love one another. It also requires an understanding of the Biblical roles of each partner. When these are out of balance problems arise.

These issues can make life very difficult. My wife and I have both fallen into the traps that Jim reveals in his book. I've experienced firsthand the consequences of being a passive husband, the topic of this new book by Jim Lange. It's a topic that has been hidden under the rug for far too long.

In my marriage, I continued in my passivity while my wife was controlling. Thankfully, we resolved those issues, and we remain happily married. My wife and I both had to address control and passivity in our respective roles. It wasn't easy, but we're both better for it today. The Bible says "The truth shall make you free." When you learn the truth about your issues, it becomes the entry door to healing in your life.

Are you stuck in a tough marriage? Do you live in a relationship in which you're being dominated? Or perhaps you're the dominant person. If either of these scenarios describes your situation, this book is for you.

We live in a culture that propagates unhealthy male-female relationships and stereotypes of men that are often accepted even in the Church. When the marriage roles lose their balance, marriage becomes very difficult. And both partners suffer.

We all carry baggage into our marriages because we are born into a broken world. This baggage can be very destructive to us and our marriages if not dealt with.

When one partner is dominant and the other is passive, this creates a painful existence for both, especially the passive partner. Consider the story of Jezebel and Ahab in the Old Testament. Jezebel was a controlling queen married to Ahab, a passive King. They were quite the dysfunctional power couple.

Jezebels are controllers who want to dominate their partners emotionally, spiritually, and physically. The most common reason Jezebels become Jezebels is a wounded heart in their childhood. They grew up thinking they must protect themselves at all costs, which, to them, means controlling the people and the circumstances around them.

Ahabs, on the other extreme, are passive. This book explores many of the reasons for this truth. Jezebels can't exist without an Ahab. Ahabs usually have a stronghold of insecurity and fear that makes them appease their Jezebel for the sake of peace. Keeping the peace in their marriages becomes more important to them than breaking the cycle of control and passivity. This leaves them at the mercy of Jezebel which can bring disaster.

In *The Happy Wife, Happy Life Deception*, Jim addresses the devastating impact of men living as passive leaders in the home. He digs to the root, presents a balanced understanding of the underlying issues, and exposes common misconceptions of how men are to truly lead in their families.

Yet, he doesn't label women as being the problem. Instead, he demonstrates how culture has developed stereotypes of what the male-female relationship should be today and how contrary it is to the biblical role of male and female in marriage.

This is a very important book and I applaud Jim for having the courage to write it. My prayer is that this book will bring real freedom to men and help them to overcome passivity and timidity. We *can* become the godly, loving, and strong men God made us to be.

~Os Hillman
Author and President, Marketplace Leaders

GETTING PERSONAL

"Doesn't my happiness mean *anything* to you?" Melody snapped. Jeff blinked at her, flabbergasted. To hear those words from his wife's mouth, and laced with so much venom, rocked him to his core.

"Your happiness means *everything* to me!" he replied. "I do everything I can to make sure you're happy."

Melody scoffed and folded her arms. "That's a laugh."

"Why are you saying that?" Jeff asked. "You don't think it's true?"

"If my happiness were really important to you, and if you loved me, your behavior would be different. A *lot* different."

"Tell me what you want me to do, and I'll do it," Jeff pleaded. He meant every word of it. From his perspective, he'd worked their entire marriage to ensure her happiness. That's what he was trying to do this very moment.

"Do you expect me to write you a list?" Melody shook her head. "You should *know* what I want. You're my husband."

"Melody, I'm sitting with you right now, listening. I can't read your mind. If you tell me what you want me to change, I'll change it right now."

"And when has that ever worked in the past? I've told you all of this before, and nothing has changed."

For the first time in the conversation, Jeff agreed with her. They'd been here before, and now they were here again. He'd tried to do what she'd asked every other time they'd had this argument, but it never made a lasting difference. They just ended up in yet another shouting match.

"Fine. You want a list? I'll give you one." Melody held out her hand and pointed to her fingers as she recited her grievances. "You don't spend enough time with me. You're overly critical of me. You have a stranglehold on our finances. You don't treat me the way a Christian man is supposed to treat his wife."

"What does that mean?" Jeff interjected.

Melody continued, "And you interrupt me when I'm talking to you."

"I'm sorry," Jeff said. "You're right. I just need clarification on some of these things."

"You know *exactly* what I mean, Jeff," she fired back. "I'm done talking about this. Maybe you should go pray about how you can be a better husband. I'm not going to have this argument anymore."

Jeff shuddered. *What does she mean by that?*

As Melody picked up the TV remote and clicked it on, Jeff gulped back his emotions. He stood and walked out of the room, defeated.

"I just don't know what to do anymore," Jeff said to Nick, his mentor, while fighting back tears.

He'd already cried plenty over the last 36 hours, and even though he trusted Nick more than just about anyone, he didn't want to look weak. Call it a male-pride thing, or whatever, but he'd endured enough emasculation as of late.

"It seems like no matter what I do, I can't seem to make her happy," Jeff continued. "She just wants more, more, more. I do my best to give it to her, but it's impossible."

Nick sipped his coffee, listening. "What else is she asking for?"

Jeff rattled off Melody's list for him. "I've already given up most of my hobbies, my friends, and my interests so I can spend more time with her. I try not to be critical of her because I know she hates when I do that, but now we can hardly even have a serious conversation without it becoming an argument. She seems to take everything I say as a personal attack, even though I don't mean for it to come across that way.

"I let her spend more money than I should because it makes her happy and because it helps me avoid an argument, but then whenever I ask her to scale back, that starts a fight, and she accuses me of being cheap. And she wants me to treat her 'the way a Christian man is supposed to treat his wife,'" Jeff continued. "I try to do that every day, and most days, I think I do a great job of it."

"But she doesn't seem to think so?" Nick asked.

Jeff shook his head and inhaled a long, solemn breath to calm his quaking nerves. "No. But she won't tell me what that means, either. Or at least, what *she* thinks it means. I'm no stranger to the Bible. I've studied its teachings on marriage, and I'm doing my best to use the Bible as the standard by which I judge my marriage."

"Let me ask you something." Nick leaned forward. "And I don't mean to insult you in asking this…"

Jeff trusted Nick, but the conversation's new direction started to worry him.

"…but have you ever considered that you've been abused in your marriage?"

Jeff blinked at Nick. "That's crazy talk."

"I know it may sound strange, but I'm being serious," Nick continued. "Have you ever considered it?"

Jeff shook his head. "No, but that's because it doesn't make any sense."

"From what you've told me, I think it fits perfectly."

"How?"

"You've told me that Melody repeatedly swears at you, calls you names, and even withholds sex as a punishment."

Jeff winced at that one. His self-esteem took a huge hit whenever that came up.

As of this morning, he and Melody hadn't had sex for 37 days. He felt miserable, unloved and like a total failure as a man.

I fully committed myself to be faithful to this woman. Her and no other. I honored her with that. And she throws it all in the trash. Sex means everything to me, but apparently it means nothing to her. I feel like I got the "bait and switch" early in our marriage I never imagined she could turn this cold. I feel so alone.

Nick folded his hands on the table and interrupted Jeff's thoughts. "You've also told me she's very controlling. When you consider that, along with all the other things I just mentioned, it sounds more and more like abuse, Jeff."

It can't be. Melody's not abusing me, is she? Jeff leaned back in his chair.

"Look, I know it may be hard to see from your perspective. You love her, want the best for her, and want to make her happy. I get that." Nick cupped his hands around his mug of coffee again. "But the reality is that functioning marriages don't include those behaviors, and certainly not with the regularity you're seeing in your marriage."

Jeff folded his arms. He didn't want to hear this, but maybe Nick was right.

"You've told me you feel hopeless and disrespected. I'm guessing you also feel weak and like a failure. Am I right, Jeff? The list goes on from there, right?"

Jeff nodded. It was true.

"And you admit that you've been trying harder and harder after each one of these fights to make Melody happy?"

"Yes, always. But she doesn't see it." *Or she doesn't care to.*

"Then maybe it's time to consider that you're going about things the wrong way," Nick said. "Maybe it's time to stop putting your wife's happiness first."

Jeff couldn't believe what he'd just heard. Was Nick actually suggesting that Melody's happiness wasn't as important as he'd been making it?

He'd known and trusted Nick for years. Nick had counseled him through a lot of difficult times, and Jeff remained truly thankful to him for everything, but most of Nick's other advice had made sense. This suggestion did not.

But as Jeff gave Nick's words more consideration, they began to resonate with something deep inside of him. Everything he'd been doing wasn't working. In fact, things had only gotten worse.

Maybe it was time for a new kind of change.

"Okay." Jeff placed his palms flat on the table. "What do you think I should do?"

Jeff's story is not an isolated one. Unfortunately, it plays out repeatedly in the homes of men throughout the world and even in the lives of respected pastors and other godly leaders.

I empathize with Jeff because I, too, have battled passivity and timidity for most of my life. Through the extensive work I do with leaders and hurting men, I have come to realize this is an epidemic in our culture, and especially in Christian men.

Passivity

When I mention passivity, I don't mean the act of pursuing nothing. Each of us pursues something, even if it's selfish or destructive.

What I mean is that we often pursue something other than what God desires for us. He has designed each of us to pursue Him and to walk in His ways. When we don't do this, we are often passive (or rebellious and disobedient).

A few examples of passivity include:

- Remaining silent to avoid conflict
- Abdicating responsibility
- Not confronting sin in the lives of others, including your wife (and yourself)
- Not encouraging others, including your wife and children

Many men can't see that they're passive and timid because they expend great effort to improve things in their marriages and families. *It doesn't seem possible that someone who's working so hard could be passive and timid.*

As we will discover, passivity has nothing to do with laziness.

Typical behavior of abusive men takes many forms: alcoholism, porn addiction, physical abuse, cheating, etc. However, passive men can be equally destructive; they not only cause damage to themselves but also to those around them, most notably their wives and children.

This book examines the reasons passivity is a prevalent issue with today's men. We'll examine our culture and the Church. We'll also look at why our wives and others[1] might treat us this way, and then we'll look at what's going on within us—or "under the hood."

Lastly, we'll walk through several strategies to help us stop walking on eggshells and regain the lives that God has planned for us.

But first, let's look at what it means to live as a man.

Biblical Manhood

There are some really good resources[2] that paint a clear picture of what it means to be a true man through the lens of Scripture, so I'm not going to rewrite what has already been written. Rather, let's review a brief summary of what biblical manhood looks like.

By contrasting the lives of the first Adam (Adam) and the second

Adam (Jesus), Robert Lewis[3] identified four attributes which define a true biblical man. A true man does as Jesus did and...

- **Rejects passivity**—Instead of standing by and letting life "happen" to him, a true man rejects that passivity and initiates in a sacrificial way.
- **Accepts responsibility**—A true man understands that he is to obey God, and that he has a work to do. Jesus said this to His Father in John 17:4, "I have brought you glory on earth by completing the work you gave me to do." We are called to work and a true man does his work well knowing it brings glory to God. He also cares for and protects his wife (just as Jesus cares for and protects His bride—the Church, which is us).
- **Leads courageously**—A true man says, "Follow me because I follow Jesus," and he leads his followers into noble pursuits.
- **Expects the greater reward—God's reward**—True men invest eternally instead of choosing the forbidden fruit lingering in front of them in the moment. In other words, true men exhibit self-control.

This template is not only biblical but also simple and applicable to any man. Whether you're a computer programmer, an outdoorsman, or both, these principles still apply.

> No matter our differences... each of us has been given a noble calling to be a true man.

Let's discover some of the things that can so easily move us toward passivity and further from authentic manhood. Before we do, I'm going to pray for you, and then share a confession with you.

A prayer for you:

Father, I'm so thankful for my friend who is reading this now. I pray that you would open his eyes. I pray that you would help him not to feel so alone and that he would find comfort in the coming pages.

Father, please encourage Your son... he's so weary and burdened. I ache for him and the pain he's suffering, and I know You do as well. Please help him to experience You in new ways, Lord.

And finally, I pray that You would release him from the chains that have bound him for so long. Amen.

[2]

MY CONFESSION

Without a doubt, the last 15 years have been the toughest of my life. And the past 5, absolutely gut-wrenching.

Though I've sometimes blamed others for my tribulations, there is only one person to blame. Me.

Never in my wildest dreams did I envision that I would get divorced. In fact, I often said to my wife that divorce was not an option. Yet after 30 years of marriage, I am now divorced.

It would be easy for me to blame my former wife, my circumstances, or global warming. But that would conveniently avoid the root cause—the stuff going on inside of me.

For years, I thought we had an amazing marriage and that I was a godly husband. I was practically breaking my arm patting myself on the back.

But there were unseen cracks in the foundation of our marriage caused primarily by my passivity and timidity—and I discovered this was not God's way for men.

It wasn't until much later in my marriage that I came to realize that I had confused *honoring my wife* with *passivity and timidity*. I'm embarrassed to admit that for over 20 years I didn't even know I was passive and timid.

I thought I was a biblical role-model of a husband. Looking back, I now realize that I listened to some well-meaning people whose bad advice only deepened my deception.

I now know that I wasn't honoring God. Certainly, both of us contributed to the breakup of our marriage; however, I feel primarily responsible because I let passivity and timidity reign in my life for decades. That passivity enabled the erosion of our marriage.

Memories and Paying the Price

My divorce affected me deeply in my body, soul, and spirit.

From the perspective of my body, I was diagnosed with adrenal fatigue which lasted more than two years after our divorce. I was exhausted all the time (which didn't help my emotional state). At times it was so bad that I'd felt as if I'd been run over by a truck.

My soul (my mind, will, and emotions) felt completely broken and overwhelmed. I was running on empty and no longer felt like a real man.

My spirit also endured serious wounds, and I felt like a second-class Christian around certain "church people"— like some sort of an outcast.

My hopes and dreams for our marriage shattered, and I experienced a depth of grief that I'd never experienced before—or since. And I want to help men, and women, avoid this pain.

While the decay of our marriage was sad and extremely difficult, I can honestly say that I'm so thankful for my former wife and the fact that we were married for 30 years.

We have some tremendous memories together. We have three amazing children—and now grandchildren. She was—and still is—a terrific mom.

And I've learned so much about myself. I've become more whole as a person because of our marriage—and because of our divorce. Though we couldn't salvage our marriage, I'm a better man because I was married to her.

The Question You Should Be Asking

If he's divorced, why should I listen to him?

This is an excellent question.

Over the past decade, men have continually approached me to discuss their marital situations—and most of the time they knew nothing of my story.

It's as if they're attracted to me like metal filings to a magnet. I can't explain it any other way other than to say that I know God has called me to help such men.

Whenever a man tells me of his marital challenges, my heart aches for him and his wife. I understand his pain and loneliness. I long to help him find freedom from the lies that have bound him and, hopefully, help him to rebuild his marriage on a solid foundation.

Here are some of the ways in which God has equipped me to be a valuable asset to people in these situations.

First, I have coached (marital coaching, business coaching, executive roundtable coaching, etc.) many people from all walks of life including executives and business owners leading companies of all sizes to pastors, non-profit leaders, and even college students. In the past decade I've begun using my coaching expertise to guide men through difficult waters, especially in their marriages.

Second, through the difficulties in my own marriage, I've learned a tremendous amount. For 15 years I read countless books and did endless research, listened to dozens of podcasts and interviewed many experts on ways to find healing and freedom.

In addition, through this process, I've found a new level of freedom from the false beliefs which led me to unhealthy behaviors in my marriage. I now have a level of peace I never thought possible, and I experience great joy in helping others find this same freedom.

I've made many significant mistakes along the way, and it's a profound blessing to give men the wisdom and tools to help them avoid the errors I made.

Much of what I've learned and experienced personally, and with my coaching clients, has been synthesized in this book.

In the pages that follow, I share stories from the lives of many men and women struggling in their marriages (all names have been changed). Some of these stories result in restored marriages; some end in failed marriages.

But in each case, the men in the stories have restored souls—or souls in the process of restoration—and have achieved much greater peace.

An important point however, is that the outcomes of the marriages in each of these stories do not define success. Am I hoping and praying your marriage turns around? Yes.

However, in my case, I was acting in a timid way by walking on eggshells in order to maintain a false peace (settling for the status quo because, though it was not great, it was better than greater conflict). By doing so, I was attempting to control the harmony in our marriage. In other words, I was trying to do what only God can do— control outcomes.

Controlling outcomes is one way to make an idol of something. I realized that I had made an idol out of my marriage. I had put it above God and how He was leading me to behave. This led me to act as a peacekeeper, rather than a peacemaker.

In His Sermon on the Mount (Matthew 5), Jesus says, "Blessed are the peace*makers*, for they will be called sons of God." (Matthew 5:9, emphasis added)

Peacemakers are willing to do hard things to make true peace. Peacekeepers, on the other hand, simply try to maintain the current level of peace, even if it's a false peace. I was a peacekeeper.

In my personal experience, and in my work with other men, I've discovered that the best chance a man has of restoring his marriage is for him to grow and heal.

You can only control your own soul and your own actions. Becoming the best version of yourself is the best thing you can do for your wife, your kids, your marriage, and yourself.

Who is This For?

This book is not about focusing on any woman or group of women.

This is about men who are willing to focus on themselves, recognize their deficiencies, and get healthy in all areas of their lives.

It's dangerous to try to assign blame when things are going sideways in a relationship because this means we're focusing on the other person's "stuff," at least to some extent. In reality, we can only deal with our side of the street, so focusing on ourselves is the only prudent thing to do.

And as you will see, this is the best way—and perhaps the only way—to possibly restore your marriage and begin to honor God in your marital relationship.

If you're reading this in hopes of finding a reason to blame your wife—or someone else—this book is not for you.

On the other hand, if you want answers and real help with your "stuff," then read on—I believe you will be challenged and blessed.

Let's explore some of the things that push men toward passivity and pull them away from authentic manhood.

[3]
THE EPIDEMIC OF PASSIVITY: EXTERNAL
CONTRIBUTORS

"A nation or civilization that continues to produce soft-minded men
purchases its own spiritual death on the installment plan."
~Martin Luther King Jr.

I recently attended a meeting with 12 respected, accomplished
leaders. In the group were 10 men and 2 women. During our
weekend together we learned a lot about one another.

At one point, several in the room began to speak into my life
regarding the things God was showing them and the things they saw
in me. They began to share with me that it was apparent to them that
I had battled passivity and timidity. One of the men said, "I've battled
that same thing."

As we broke for lunch, two young men in the group approached
me and one of them stated, "I've dealt with that very thing in my
relationship with my girlfriend."

The other said, "I also fear conflict in my marriage, but thankfully
my wife doesn't."

I asked the married one a few questions, and he came to the
realization that he battled timidity as well. I took the opportunity to

pray with and encourage them with some of the same wisdom I will share with you in the following chapters.

In this group of 12 leaders, 10 were men. And of those 10, at least 4 of us had battled passivity and timidity in our relationships, particularly with the woman in our lives.

Everywhere I go to speak, men approach me to tell me, "You have no idea how much I needed to hear this message today. This is the first time I feel like someone understands what I've been dealing with."

I also see these passive and timid tendencies in friends, acquaintances, and clients.

OVER TIME, I HAVE COME TO SEE THAT PASSIVITY AND TIMIDITY
IN MEN IS AN EPIDEMIC—ESPECIALLY AMONG CHRISTIANS.

A Story of Two Leaders (Ken & James)

Ken is a business and community leader. He's well-respected by everyone—well... *almost* everyone.

At home he's relegated to a life of silence... and pain. His wife is extremely judgmental, of him and others, and very controlling. Over time, Ken has lost his voice and has become emasculated.

Ken's story contains a number of troubling aspects; perhaps most disturbing is the fact that Ken is unaware of his problem.

James has been a pastor at the same church for many years. His congregation thinks the world of him.

Yet at home, he lives in a prison. He is weary and fearful of his wife, and he feels trapped. Nobody, including those in his congregation, suspects a thing—in fact, most of the flock has put the couple on a pedestal as a picture of a godly marriage.

James admits that if he confronts his wife—or tries to change things—it would be very painful and could lead to divorce. This is unthinkable for James since it might lead to the loss of his church. He says, "I feel so trapped and so alone."

How can a grown man (Ken)—a well-respected leader—not see what's happening in his home as a problem?

How can a pastor (James) be stuck in this place of fear?

How is it that so many men today, potentially millions, are trapped in this prison of passivity and timidity?

Both external and internal factors contribute to this epidemic. We will briefly discuss some external influences in Chapter 3 and Chapter 4, and then we'll address the internal factors in Chapter 5.

Contributors | Historical

A couple of events in our history have driven men toward passivity.

Industrial Revolution

Before the Industrial Revolution, sons used to hang out with their fathers working in the fields. After the Industrial Revolution, many fathers went off to work where they could no longer be with their sons during the day. Then when they came home, they were exhausted and not able to sow into their sons the way they once did.[1]

As a result, women became the primary care-givers. In some respects, this is a wonderful thing.

However, sons need time with their fathers in order to learn what it means to live as a man (see Ephesians 6:4). Because today's fathers weren't taught this when they were growing up, even if they do have the time to sow into their sons' lives, what they impart is typically not true manhood.

War

Then came a century of wars. Many fathers never came home, and those who were fortunate enough to return often came back emotionally-scarred.

Though PTSD was not a term used during that time, many who returned from war certainly suffered from its affects. The National Center for PTSD (US Department of Veterans Affairs) has estimated that about 30% of the men and women who have spent time in war zones experience PTSD.[2]

Combat-caused PTSD is today—and was in wars past—a primary contributor to psychiatric disorders including depression, alcohol and drug abuse, phobias, panic disorders and psychosomatic and psychotic disorders.[3] Because of this, many of the men who returned from the wars of the 20th century were incapable of being emotionally present. As a result, many sons were left to figure out manhood on their own.

Contributors | Culture

When was the last time you watched a television sitcom in which the husband/father didn't look like a boob or a weak leader? In most, if not all, of these shows, it is the wife/mother who is the wise, cool, smart family leader.

Consider these sitcom couples:

- Homer and Marge Simpson from *The Simpsons*
- Peter and Lois Griffin from *Family Guy*
- Ray and Debra Barone from *Everyone Loves Raymond*
- Phil and Claire Dunphy in *Modern Family*
- Tim and Jill Taylor in *Home Improvement*
- Bill and Judy Miller in *Still Standing*
- Hal and Lois Wilkerson in *Malcolm in the Middle*
- Brock and Reba Hart in *Reba*

Even in shows where the men are not married or were not shown with their wives, they appear foolish, spineless, careless, and weak. Think about the men on *Seinfeld*, the men on *Friends*, and Norm, Cliff, and their pals on *Cheers*.

As much as we don't want to admit it, these influences change culture, especially since these shows repeatedly promote similar messages.

I understand how Ken (mentioned earlier in this chapter) might think that it's okay that his wife controls him and walks all over him —that's exactly what our culture teaches us.

Contributors | Philosophy of Manhood

Men Can't be Abused?

Our culture minimizes emotions in men.[4] Our boys learn to just "suck it up" and not be emotional. In other words, *real men don't get emotional, and real men don't get hurt.*

As a result, men who endure abusive relationships are reluctant to discuss this with anyone in order to not appear weak and unmanly.

Men might also fear that others won't believe them. After all...

WHEN'S THE LAST TIME YOU HEARD OF A HUSBAND BEING ABUSED?
HAVE YOU EVER HEARD OF A BATTERED HUSBAND SHELTER?

Culture almost always universally communicates that abuse is from husband to wife. If something *is* reported about a wife abusing a husband, it is typically treated as a laughing matter.

The Guy is the Issue?

Another cultural reality is that in most marital issues, it is the man who is usually assumed to be at fault.

A coaching client named Tony told me, "My wife and I have been to three counselors. At the beginning with each, it's been assumed that I'm the problem. I'm sure it's because I'm the man. It also seems that anyone in our church who hears that we're having difficulties assumes that I'm the one causing them."

Shawn said, "My wife would get me in a corner and repeatedly beat me with the sharp heel of her high-heeled shoes. Many times, I would bleed profusely. I felt that I couldn't fight back because she would threaten to call the police the instant I did.

"My attorney informed me that I should stay away from her while in the house. His concern was that she might brush my shoulder, fall over, claim abuse, and call the police. He assured me that, should this happen, I'd be thrown in jail without question regardless of my innocence. It's so sad that husbands are always assumed to be the guilty party."

When a man is physically or emotionally abused, who can he tell? As Tony observed, even some counselors unconsciously assume that the husband is the one most at fault.

For a man to claim abuse of any type, he worries about appearances. As Roy explained, "I'm 6'4" and weigh 250 pounds. My wife is 5'4" and weighs 125 pounds. How can I tell anyone that she's abusing me and that I'm actually afraid of her? It seems so pitiful and weak!"

Roy continued, "I'm dying for some help and have been looking for resources to address this. But all I seem to find are books for women trapped in abusive relationships and marriage books that tell me I'm the problem. Even my pastor doesn't seem to believe me. I don't know what to do."

Contributors | The Church

Headship Confusion

Wives, submit to your husbands as to the Lord. For the husband is the head of

the wife as Christ is the head of the church, his body, of which he is the
Savior.
    ~ Ephesians 5:22–23

This is one of the most controversial verses in the Bible, and it's often misunderstood. Some church leaders even avoid teaching on this passage.

In the verse above, many men and women have unknowingly interpreted "head" or "headship" as meaning "a controlling dictator" or "to lord over someone"—in this case, as a husband over a wife. Unfortunately, this has led to extremely abusive behavior in some men—toward women and others—for much of human history. This is not the intent of this verse.

In this case, the word "head," does not mean to "rule over." Rather, it indicates a special responsibility for the husband that parallels Christ's ministry to His Church. This is to be exhibited by the husband through leadership and caring.

I love how this commentary unpacks this passage: "...such submission [by the wife to the husband] now (1) was to be done for the sake of the Lord (v. 22) and (2) was balanced by the love of the husband even to the point of self-sacrifice (v. 25). It is striking that there is no command here for the husband to rule his wife. His only instruction is to love and care for her. The husband should not claim authority over his wife the way a Roman used to."[5]

Though the man is clearly not meant to rule over his wife like a king, the fact is that he is called to be the initiator, or leader, of her and his family. Men have been given this authority—and responsibility—by God.

Imagine being in downtown Manhattan on a Friday afternoon after a car accident has taken place. A policeman stands in the intersection directing traffic, and the drivers obey him, turning a chaotic and unsafe situation into a manageable event.

Now imagine that same policeman is placed in the intersection without his uniform, badge, and gun, and is told to direct traffic. Will the scene be as safe? Of course not.

Few would obey or listen to his instructions because he has been stripped of his authority—at least in the eyes of the drivers. As a result, he wouldn't be able to protect the people he so desires to protect.

Granted, that same policeman could also use his power and authority to harm others, but most officers join the police to "serve and protect."

THE SAME THING HAPPENS WHEN A MAN ABDICATES HIS ROLE AS THE HEAD OF HIS WIFE. HE NO LONGER HAS THE AUTHORITY TO DEFEND HER, TO PROTECT HER, TO BRING GOOD TO HER, OR EVEN TO LOVE HER FULLY.

When we as men fail to take responsibility as the "head," we disobey and dishonor God, and we fail to lead, protect, and love our wives the way God intended. However, *how* we lead is of utmost importance.

A MAN CAN'T BE WHO HIS WIFE DESIRES IF HE ABUSES HIS AUTHORITY *OR* IF HE ALLOWS HER TO STRIP HIM OF HIS AUTHORITY.

Many Christian men (and women) have slowly adopted these passive beliefs and this bad theology. And church leaders are sometimes ill-equipped to teach these important masculine roles taught by scripture.

Theology of Masculine Passivity

In this section I will be focused on the importance of having a balanced view of God's characteristics. God has attributes that seem feminine to many Christians (e.g. love, gentleness, grace, mercy), and He has attributes that seem more masculine (e.g. powerful, strong, assertive). The problem occurs when the scale tips too much to either side.

For generations, many men have incorrectly used the teachings of the Church and focused primarily on God's "masculine" attributes to justify their abusiveness. However, it seems the scale has tipped too far the other way in recent decades with certain men.

I love the Church. We are the Church. Christ is the head of the Church. I believe strongly in its call and its redemptive power. But it's important to follow Christ's teaching on the "head" to make sure we aren't participating in inadvertently leading men toward lives of passivity and timidity, especially in their marriages.

I once spoke at a men's breakfast to approximately 60 men. As I began, I asked them to shout out attributes of God and I wrote them on the white-board. After writing 15 of them, I stopped.

Here's what I had written down:

- LOVING
- COMPASSIONATE
- TEACHER
- CARING
- GRACEFUL
- FAITHFUL
- GENTLE
- ALMIGHTY
- INTENTIONAL
- FORGIVING
- OMNIPRESENT
- MERCIFUL
- JUST
- FRIEND
- GOOD

I then asked them to tell me which traits they felt were more masculine and which they felt were more feminine.

We went through each of them and this is how this group of men categorized them:

- LOVING (F)
- COMPASSIONATE (F)
- TEACHER (F)
- CARING (F)
- GRACEFUL (F)
- FAITHFUL (F)
- GENTLE (F)
- ALMIGHTY (M)
- INTENTIONAL (M)
- FORGIVING (F)
- OMNIPRESENT (F)
- MERCIFUL (F)
- JUST (M)
- FRIEND (F)
- GOOD (F)

We could argue about how they categorized these, but that's not the point. It shows that when a group of men were asked to name attributes of their Heavenly Father, they named mostly attributes that *they* considered to be feminine (12 vs. 3 in this case).

The unbalanced nature of the attributes of God listed by this group of men illustrates their skewed view of God. If we're wrong about God, we'll also be wrong about ourselves.

In this corner: Grace
In the other corner: ?

Another contributor is the strong emphasis many churches place on God's grace, sometimes at the expense of God's truth.

To be clear, it is not possible to emphasize God's grace enough.
If we are a child of God, we can never be more
righteous than the moment we make that decision.
(See Chapter 14 for more on this.)

We cannot earn God's grace. However, if we only focus on grace and don't teach with a similar intentionality about His truth, men (and everyone else) can develop a warped sense of who God fully is.

I am not implying that men are not to be loving, kind, caring, gentle, full of grace, etc. We should be all of these!

My point is that it seems men are coaxed into believing that they should not behave as true men. Worse still, they're taught that there's something *wrong* with behaving as real men. This, combined with a lack of focus on God's truth, can contribute to men behaving in a passive and timid way.

In this corner: Grace
In the other corner: TRUTH

Jesus personified both grace *and* truth (see John 1:17). Author Henry Cloud says,

> "Truth without grace can be called judgment. Grace without truth can be named license."

In other words, when we focus on one more than the other it will lead to problems in our lives. Focusing too heavily on the "truth" side will cause us to be more judgmental. And if we lean too far in the "grace" direction then it can seem that we are giving others permission to do whatever they want, even if it hurts us.

I believe that this unintentional hyper-focus on grace (at the expense of truth) gives license—or permission—to some men and women to not live out the roles God designed for them.

Marriage Books

I've read dozens of books on marriage and am astounded by how many imply that if the husband would just love his wife more, the marriage would be much better.

There *is* truth to this general statement because if a man loves his wife more, their marriage typically will improve. However, what's missing in these books is a depiction of what love really looks like.

Normally, marriage books suggest that the man should love his wife in ways such as these:

- Spending more time with her
- Going on date nights with her
- Helping with house work
- Surprising her with flowers
- Planning romantic evenings
- Giving her random hugs and telling her how beautiful she looks with no agenda
- Holding her hand
- Listening and not trying to fix her

These are all wonderful things. But if this is the *only* picture of love that the man has, and if he's in a destructive relationship, he's headed for catastrophe.

Consider John. He'd been married to Kate for 20 years, and he'd been a Christian for 17 of those years.

In a discussion about his struggles with his wise and trusted friend, Felix, he said, "I know that, as a Christian, I'm called to love God and love others. So I've tried my best to love God to the best of my ability and do the same with others, especially my wife.

"I've scheduled date nights and romantic evenings. I've even scheduled the babysitters. I've given up more and more of the things I like to do because Kate says she wants more of my time."

Having lived through a very similar pattern in his own marriage, Felix nodded, so John continued.

"The strange thing is, the more I give, the worse it seems to get. We're becoming more distant—and she grows more critical. I've read marriage book after marriage book, and I've tried to follow everything the authors say I need to do. I figured I still wasn't doing things right—so I need to just try harder. But this isn't working, so I'm questioning everything."

Felix said, "John, when I was navigating very similar waters in my own marriage a decade ago, I was doing the same thing as you... trying harder only to see things get worse. Then my mentor spoke truth that I desperately needed to hear: 'You're being deceived.'

"So now, I'm going to tell you the same thing: I believe you're being deceived. Many consider that *Love God, Love Others* summarizes the Bible. It sounds really nice and true, but it's not *entirely* true. *Love God, Love Yourself, Love Others* is more accurate. It's really *six* words that summarize the Bible."

He continued, "Jesus said that we're to love others as we love ourselves, right?"

John nodded.

"Certainly some people love themselves in a narcissistic kind of way, which is not good. But if you're not showing appropriate love to yourself, according to Jesus, you're not able to show true love to Kate. And based on what you've been telling me, it appears you haven't been showing love to yourself."

Stunned, John asked, "How have I not been showing love to myself?"

"You've given up things that energize you and give you life, and you've allowed her to do hurtful things to you—all because you think that's the 'loving' thing to do. That's not love—at least not the love that Jesus describes.

"This is the best thing I did to help me find freedom. I started caring for myself. It not only helped me, but it actually helped to restore our marriage. You need to do the same. You need to give yourself permission to start loving yourself, man! Start caring for *you*."

That day marked a huge paradigm shift for John as he realized that he'd subscribed to a deception—one that sounded so true *and* biblical.

This is critical for us to understand as well. Jesus tells us to love others *as* we love ourselves.

> WE CAN ONLY LOVE OTHERS TO THE
> EXTENT THAT WE LOVE OURSELVES.

Because of the harmful things he allowed his wife to do to him, John was not showing love to himself. Therefore, according to Jesus, he wasn't capable of loving his wife appropriately.

Unfortunately, John's story is not unique. I've talked to numerous men who have told me similar things.

> THESE SUBTLE HALF-TRUTHS THAT ARE TAUGHT, SAID, AND WRITTEN
> ABOUT CAN BE VERY INFLUENTIAL IN OUR LIVES IF WE ARE NOT
> DISCERNING.

Mother's Day/Father's Day

In my years of attending church, I've realized that on Mother's Day, moms are typically honored from the pulpit and told how wonderful and amazing they are (which is true). However, this day often becomes an opportunity to bash men or make fun of them, and we may not even be aware of the damage this can cause.

I once attended a church service on Mother's Day in which mothers were honored and men were bashed. I'm sure the pastor meant no ill-intent, but he shared this quote from Margaret Thatcher while making a point about all the things women do, "If you want something said, ask a man; if you want something done, ask a woman."

In other words, "Men can't be counted on."

On the flip-side, the Father's Day message is often how men need to step it up, be better leaders, and love their wives and children more. Certainly, this is true for many of us; however, I've never heard a message on Mother's Day talking about how the women need to be better or do more.

It's so easy for church leaders to unknowingly go along with culture and tear down men, not understanding the damage this does to them. I used to buy in to this rhetoric, thinking that I just needed to suck it up and do more and be better.

Men are inundated with messages (even from the Church) of how we don't measure up and how we're not doing enough. If we aren't discerning, this influx of bad information results in unhealthy beliefs, behavior, and relationships.

Now we'll explore a few other factors that have contributed to passivity in men.

THE EPIDEMIC OF PASSIVITY: OTHER FACTORS

The Church inadvertently propagates some other harmful ideas:

Healthy Conflict? | The Value of Marriage

The Church rightfully puts a high value on marriage—God clearly does as well.

However, how often have you heard from the pulpit a message about what to do when there is abuse in a marriage (verbal, physical, emotional, spiritual, sexual, etc.)? Or how to have a difficult conversation in your marriage? In the rare instance when something like this is discussed, have you ever heard about the possibility of a husband being abused?

Because of the complexity of such topics and concepts, I understand why they're difficult to discuss. I can see how discussing these things might make it appear that the Church is not strong on marriage.

Many couples are dying in their marriages and are looking for any guidance they can find. But because it's difficult to address, because it has become the norm, because of the fear of man (e.g. people-pleasing and doing things because of how someone will view us, rather than fearing God alone), and for other reasons, the Church has been largely silent on this topic.

Again, I get it. This is a difficult thing to discuss because a pastor wouldn't want to give the impression that divorce is ever an option. However, when it isn't addressed, wives and husbands may not assert themselves, leaving many couples rudderless.

THIS AVOIDANCE CAN
ACTUALLY LEAD TO DIVORCE.

Loving Our Wives As Christ Loved the Church

Most men's groups I've participated in, talk about how we are to love our wives as Christ loved the Church (see Ephesians 5:25). The implication is that we are to lay our lives down for our wives.

As husbands we are called to sacrifice; however, I believe many men are taught to misapply this principle in their lives.

AS A RESULT, MEN OFTEN INCORRECTLY BELIEVE THAT
THEY ARE TO SACRIFICE UNDER *ALL* CIRCUMSTANCES,
EVEN IF IT MEANS ALLOWING BEHAVIORS THAT BRING HARM TO THEM.

However, Jesus clearly told us that we are to love others *as we love ourselves.*

When Jesus instructs us to love others, we must keep in mind that we must love ourselves the way that He commands. When we allow harm to come to us we are not loving ourselves, which means we are not able to appropriately love others—including our wives— according to Jesus.

Professor Jordan B. Peterson[1] said this:

"To sacrifice ourselves to God (to the highest good, if you like) does not mean to suffer silently and willingly when some person or organization demands more from us, consistently, than is offered in return... If I am someone's friend, family member, or lover, then I am morally obliged to bargain as hard on my own behalf as they are on theirs. If I fail to do so, I will end up a slave, and the other person a tyrant. What good is that? It is much better for any relationship when both partners are strong. Furthermore, there is little difference between standing up and speaking for yourself, when you are being bullied or otherwise tormented and enslaved, and standing up and speaking for someone else... your mistreatment of yourself can have catastrophic consequences for others."

Two Types of Covenants

It is often stated that marriage is a covenant and not a contract, but this concept is often misunderstood.

The implication of a marital covenant is that when we make a decision to get married, we choose to love the other and stay with the other no matter what. This sounds good and noble and certainly seems like it would be God's view... *or is it?*

The rainbow is a reminder of God's promise to never flood the earth again:

> *I have set my rainbow in the clouds, and it will be the sign of the covenant between me and the earth.*
>
> *Whenever I bring clouds over the earth and the rainbow appears in the clouds, I will remember my covenant between me and you and all living creatures of every kind. Never again will the waters become a flood to destroy all life.*
>
> *~ Genesis 9:13–15*

This is an *unconditional* covenant... no behavior by the human race can change this promise of God.

Marriage, on the other hand, seems to be a *conditional* covenant. In the Old Testament, Israel was often referred to as God's bride (see Isaiah 54:5-6, Jeremiah 31:32).

Because of Israel's rebellion and rejection of their husband, God, He divorced His bride as indicated by the words of God:

> *"I gave faithless Israel her certificate of divorce and sent her away because of all her adulteries." ~ Jeremiah 3:8a; see also Isaiah 50:1, Ezekiel 21, Hosea 2*

But wait, *God hates divorce!* Yes, He does (see Malachi 2:16).

But is it possible that the reason God hates divorce is because of the damage it causes to those involved?

Though God divorced Israel, He still loved her deeply.

I'm not trying to encourage divorce! I'm simply pointing out what God's Word says in the hope that you will stop trying to manage or control the harmony in your marriage because of a fear of divorce. He is the only one who can control outcomes so you can trust Him—even in your difficulties.

Far too many men feel stuck and afraid to be lovingly assertive. But they're often stuck simply because they fear the idea of being divorced. They don't realize that they can't honor God and remain in a state of passivity and timidity, even though on the surface, it *feels* that staying put in their unhealthy pattern of behavior will "save" their marriage.

Once a man breaks free from this fear, he can say something like this to his wife: "I'm not willing to continue living the way we've been. We need to change."

My intent here is to illuminate and alleviate irrational fears that many of us have that can keep us stuck. We are to forgive in our marriages; however, that does not mean we need to allow our wives to harm us repeatedly.

Now let's take a look at how idol worship can play into the destruction of our marriages.

Idols?

Since the late 1970s, there seems to have been a greater focus on families in American Christianity than ever before. This has impacted millions of families worldwide in very positive ways.

But ironically, this may have also contributed to the epidemic of passivity and timidity in men.

Consider the Millennial generation (born between 1981–2002). The Millennials have much to offer society. However, I hear one complaint over and over about this group—they are "so into themselves." In other words, they want to be idolized. Is it possible that this increased focus on families has contributed to this?

Is it also possible that this emphasis on family put our marriages in the lofty place above God—as an idol in our lives?

I've known men who have inadvertently placed marriage above God (which means marriage is an idol for them). This has caused these men to behave with greater passivity and timidity—thinking they must do so to keep their marriage intact.

When we turn our marriage into an idol, we open ourselves to the possibility of being trapped in marital dysfunction because we don't know that it's okay to protect ourselves.

God cares deeply about the safety of His children. God cares as much, if not more, about you and your spouse than about the health of your marriage.

The Bible shares many examples of His children leaving dangerous situations in order to remain safe. For example:

- God warned Joseph in a dream to wake up and flee to Egypt so that young Jesus would not be killed (see Matthew 2:13).
- Jesus escaped from the Pharisees who were out to kill Him (see Matthew 12:14-16).

- David fled from Saul who was trying to kill him (see 1 Samuel 19:12; 21:10).

MANY MEN I'VE SPOKEN TO HAVE PLACED THE HEALTH OF THEIR MARRIAGE ABOVE GOD AND WHAT HE'S TELLING THEM TO DO.

I want to be clear that my reason for writing this book is to help men break free from their passivity in hopes that it will lead them and their wives into a healthy and vibrant marriage.

I'm in no way advocating for divorce. Rather, I'm focusing on the fear that passive husbands may have of divorce.

This can keep a man from wanting to "rock the boat" because he fears his marriage will further deteriorate and potentially lead to divorce. The focus in this section is to alleviate irrational fears about divorce that we have—not to give permission for divorce.

Contributors | Other Forces

"Why does she treat me this way? Why do others treat me this way?"

It would be naïve to believe that you're the *entire* problem. But you are a big part of the issue—which is good, because you can do something about your part. We'll get to that soon.

We've discussed the roles of culture and the Church, but now let's consider the roles of others, including you and your wife.

Family of Origin

The truth is that many of us haven't had healthy models of manhood to follow while growing up. Some of our fathers may not have been around at all. Other fathers or father figures who *were* there did the best they could with what they knew. Because of any number of factors, they, too, may not have had healthy models of manhood in their fathers.

In my case, I've come to realize that my mother actually had a greater impact on me in this regard. My parents were both wonderful to me while I was growing up. Did they have issues? Sure, but they were extremely loving and taught me some great values.

However, my mother had a passive streak. In reflecting back on my childhood, I can see how I inherited her fear of conflict through observing her.

Regardless of whether it came from your mother or father, in many cases, unhealthy passivity and timidity have been perpetuated in our family lines. And due to factors already mentioned, passivity seems to be increasing in each generation of men.

Wounds from The Past

I grew up in a relatively healthy two-parent home. Despite this, I still marvel at how many emotional wounds I experienced in my childhood. I've since come to understand how much these wounds have colored my world and made me see things through a distorted filter.

For example:

- Because hard work was stressed in my family and laziness looked down upon, I concluded that rest must be earned. I now know that I cannot earn rest but that God gives me rest because I'm his child (see Psalm 62:1).
- Because I was taught the importance of saving money, I interpreted that to mean that accumulating money was the key to finding peace and security. Now I grasp the reality that God is the only source of my peace and security.
- Because my basketball coaches often screamed at me when I made a mistake and sometimes praised me when I did "well," I understood that to mean that I needed to perform

to receive acceptance. I now recognize that I am acceptable simply because I am God's son, and my performance does not impact my standing with Him.

Though these wounds weren't severe for me (I'll share a more severe wound in a later chapter), they still created huge roadblocks in my mind that kept me from truth.

Having been healed from some of my wounds, the difference that wholeness has made in my life is amazing, and it has reshaped the way I feel and behave. These days I'm really excited because I continue to discover things from my past that have caused false beliefs.

This means that more and more freedom is available to me... and to you. (I'll explain more about getting free from our wounds a bit later.)

It's quite possible that part of the reason you're being treated harshly has something to do with the wounds your wife—and you— have experienced in your childhoods. I share this not so you might suggest this to her but rather to give you some understanding.

RECOMMENDATION: DON'T SUGGEST TO YOUR WIFE THAT SHE HAS WOUNDS THAT NEED HEALING—UNLESS YOU DISCERN SHE WOULD BE RECEPTIVE TO IT AND HAS EXPRESSED A WILLINGNESS TO SEEK HELP.

Spiritual Battle

We live in a spiritual battleground. The only time the enemy needs to come against you is when you threaten his kingdom. I've heard it said that if you don't have arrows coming at you, it might mean that you're heading in the same direction as the arrows.

This doesn't mean that all negative things are an attack. Jesus informed us that in this life we would have trouble (see John 16:33). Encountering negative circumstances should be expected, perhaps especially for Christ-followers.

God's Word is clear that our mistakes and sins can bring about negative consequences. This doesn't mean He loves us less or forgives us less. It means that He is a just God, and consequences are a part of the deal.

God's word is also clear that He allows difficulty in our lives for our benefit. We'll cover that more in Chapter 6.

If you are—to the best of your knowledge—walking with the Lord and have a heart of repentance (note: this doesn't mean you're perfect), you will face resistance from "our enemy."

I know this battle in your marriage is tearing your heart out. However, it's very possible that you're heading in the right direction.

Passivity Issues in Men

Our enemy is out to steal, kill, and destroy both us and our calling (see John 10:10), just as he tried to do with Jesus. One strategy Satan deploys is the sin of passivity.

In the second chapter of the Bible, Adam was created and given responsibility as well as a job—to tend and keep the garden (see Genesis 2:15). This was like leadership training before the arrival of Eve. Adam was then commanded to name the animals (see Genesis 2:19) which is evidence of his leadership calling over creation. After Eve was created (see Genesis 2:21-22) the Bible says that man—Adam in this case—is called to be the initiator (see Genesis 2:24).[2]

Then it happened:

> *When the woman saw that the fruit of the tree was good for food and pleasing to the eye, and also desirable for gaining wisdom, she took some and ate it. She also gave some to her husband, <u>who was with her</u>, and he ate it.*
> *~Genesis 3:6, emphasis added*

It's interesting that, though Eve ate of the tree first, God addresses Adam and holds him accountable (see Genesis 3:9-11). One of Adam's roles was to be the leader of creation, and his family.

Clearly, he knew that they were not to eat of this tree or they would die.

Yet this verse indicates that Adam stood by and did nothing when his bride reached for the fruit and ate it. Then—perhaps because Eve didn't die on the spot—he ate it, too.

THE FIRST SIN WAS NOT EVE'S EATING OF THE FRUIT— IT WAS ADAM'S PASSIVITY!

Many might think that Eve committed the first sin in the garden when she ate of the fruit. But it was really Adam's passivity. Perhaps he didn't want to "rock the boat" in his relationship with Eve.

No matter the reason, he remained silent, and this original sin is counted against Adam, not Eve, throughout Scripture (see Romans 5:12, 14, 19; 1 Corinthians 15:21-22).

Passivity has been around since the beginning of time and it's one of Satan's primary weapons, especially against men.

But what about women?

Let's examine a couple of reasons why women might exhibit controlling tendencies.

Character Issues in Women

Critical and controlling wives often exhibit some of these traits:

- Bitterness
- Contempt for others
- Controlling nature
- Over-criticalness
- Emotional hostility
- Pridefulness
- Spite
- Unteachable spirit/allergic to correction
- Taking credit for things; not accepting blame

- Withholding information
- Unclear communication
- Rarely giving credit or showing gratitude
- Rarely complimenting
- Rarely admitting fault
- Judgmental attitude
- Accusing others of what she herself does
- Demonstrating a know-it-all attitude
- Acting religious/pious
- Not admitting to a mistake or repenting
- Not forgiving, yet demanding forgiveness
- Being overly dramatic
- Using self-pity as a manipulative tool

An additional trait that appears fairly consistently is jealousy. It's often a subtle and unspoken jealousy that may be hard to notice or explain initially. Jealousy isn't always present, but I see it often.

Jealousy or any of the other traits above can stem from one or more of the following:

- Spiritual warfare
- Spiritual immaturity
- Physical issues (poor nutrition, lack of exercise, etc.)
- Mental issues (false beliefs, mental disorders, mental illness)
- Emotional issues (family of origin or other unresolved emotional/relational traumas)

Any of the above traits can often be tough to discern. Over time, a person becomes desensitized to these behaviors and normalizes them. It would be like asking a fish about water; the fish might reply, "What's water?"

Being married to a woman with any of these tendencies can prove difficult for a husband because the person God gave him as a helper is actually working against him.

In some cases, a wife's behavior may be symptomatic of an underlying physical or mental issue that only a qualified physician or mental health professional can properly diagnose. Let's look at one such situation.

Physical & Emotional Issues (Roger & Sara)

Roger and Sara have been married for 19 years. Roger struggled with speaking "truth" to Sara and he frequently "walked on eggshells" around her.

Sara said this frustrated her greatly, yet when Roger *would* speak truth, Sara would make him pay for it by being aggressive (mean, critical, and giving off strong emotional demonstrations) or passive-aggressive (manipulating or controlling through her moods). Over time, Roger learned it was better for him to just keep his mouth shut.

Nine years into their marriage, Sara saw a doctor who diagnosed her with a mental health issue. He prescribed a strong prescription to help her be more present and in the moment.

Once she began taking this, Roger was shocked. Sara seemed much kinder, loving, and respectful toward him. Their communication was never better. He had a new wife, and he was thrilled.

For several years this continued, and they were by far the best years of their marriage. Then Roger and Sara both committed their lives to Jesus.

Sara began to hear how God heals. She decided to pray for brain healing and began to declare that God had healed her. Instead of talking to her doctor, she decided to stop her medication.

Unfortunately for Roger, the "old" Sara promptly returned. Roger had strong faith and believed that God does heal people. However, based on his wife's behavior, it didn't appear that she was healed.

For a period of time, Roger asked Sara if she would be willing to talk with her doctor[3] about this and consider going back on her medication.

However, from his vantage point, his words would be continually squashed by Sara's angry retort, "You just lack faith!"

After three or four times, Roger stopped bringing it up and realized that this was his new marital reality.

The external factors already mentioned illustrate some of the reasons men are becoming more passive and timid in our society. Next, we'll look under the hood to discover what's going on inside of *us* that contributes to our getting stuck in this epidemic.

[5]

THE EPIDEMIC OF PASSIVITY: INTERNAL CONTRIBUTORS

W e as men have a serious problem. Culture wants us to fly upside-down by telling us we're inferior just because we're guys.

No matter where we go, it seems that we're told that we need to be more like women. As noted previously, even the Church has inadvertently contributed to this message. As a result, men are confused, and our very identity as men—as defined by God—is at stake.

However, that's not our biggest problem. Our problem is under our own hoods—inside of us.

Remember Ken and James in Chapter 3? Fear—especially fear of rejection—fueled their passivity. However, Ken and James, like frogs in water about to boil, oblivious to their impending danger, were unaware how fear had caused so much of their pain.

Often, we miss the real roots of these problems. So let's uncover some of passivity's root causes.

Insecurity

When Herod realized that he had been outwitted by the Magi, he was furious,

*and he gave orders to kill all the boys in Bethlehem and its vicinity who were
two years old and under, in accordance with the time he had learned from the
Magi.*

    ~Matthew 2:16

This is referred to as "The Slaughter of the Innocents." We don't
hear about this in Christmas carols, but it was a real event.

King Herod's insecurity led him to believe that Jesus was a threat
that needed to be eradicated. As a result, he killed all of the baby boys
in Bethlehem hoping to murder Jesus.

**THIS HAPPENED DUE TO THE BIGGEST ENEMY
OF GODLY LEADERSHIP: INSECURITY.**

Herod was a controlling and fearful leader. In my last corporate
job, I worked for a similar leader.

Out of his insecurity, this leader demeaned and overpowered
people. He removed anyone who made him look bad, opposed him,
or whom he perceived as a threat in any way.

It was the most miserable time of my career—but it led me to
write *Bleedership: Biblical First-Aid for Leaders*. As awful as this time
was, I am so thankful for it as it changed the entire trajectory of my
life.

Some people struggle with such deep insecurity that they cannot
admit when they're at fault. Consequently, they look externally for
someone or something to blame. Oftentimes insecurity is also the
source of an overbearing attitude, a critical spirit, jealousy, micro-
managing, and other relationally destructive behaviors.

The Other Side of Insecurity

Insecurity can also lead to the exact opposite behavior: passivity
and timidity.

I've exhibited this passive side of insecurity many times in my life.

Once, years ago, I took my car in to have the oil changed. They told me the car would be ready in 45 minutes.

One hour and 15 minutes later—and now late for an appointment —I approached the counter and asked, "I'm so sorry, but can you tell me how you're coming on my car?"

I was so insecure that I felt the need to apologize for asking when it was the service station employees who had not fulfilled their end of the agreement. I cringe when I think about my timidity because it characterized so much of my life.

This scenario not only plays out in the marketplace but also in millions of homes every day. (My passivity was much worse in my home, and I'll explain why in a later chapter). Many of us men have fallen prey to our insecurity and begun to believe the lie that the Church, culture, and others have been whispering in our ears: that men are the sole problem.

Sometimes the husband of an overbearing, insecure wife believes her abusive words and feels that he needs to adjust his life and simply try harder—all in an effort to please her and stop the pain.

In my work with men, I have seen that many—if not all—of our insecurities are the result of lies we believe. So let's explore several of the more pervasive lies.

THE LIES WE BELIEVE LEAD TO

MANY—IF NOT ALL—OF OUR INSECURITIES.

The Lies We Believe

Love means I'm to put up with anything (Peter & Amy)

Peter and Amy have been married for 21 years. Peter loves Amy, although she doesn't seem to accept his love. This really frustrates Peter. But that doesn't keep him from trying harder and harder to please her and make his marriage work.

Over the years, Peter has come to understand just which topics are off limits with Amy. When he crosses that line, he pays dearly for it; sometimes she bites his head off.

Other times, Amy is mean to him for long periods and sometimes withholds sex and affection[1]. Amy has even said to him before, "We could have made love tonight had you not brought up my 'spending.'"

Since Peter doesn't like conflict, and because he hates the consequences of entering into a difficult dialog with Amy (especially losing out on sex), he avoids it at all costs.

He believes that in the name of love, he is supposed to put up with all of this. He feels confident in this because of what he's read in Scripture, in books, and what he's heard from his pastor:

- We're to take up our cross daily (see Luke 9:23)
- Husbands are to love their wives as Christ loved the Church—and Christ died for the Church (see Ephesians 5:25)
- Husbands are to be considerate with their wives and treat them with respect so their prayers are not hindered (see 1 Peter 3:7)

Peter felt good about his behavior as he believed he was doing a stellar job of living up to these commands. Yet he also felt so alone and hurt because he longed for greater emotional and physical intimacy with Amy, and he wasn't receiving it.

Peter and Amy had been seeing a counselor for several years. During that time, Amy blamed Peter for all of their issues. Amy claimed to Peter and her friends that she'd been healed of all her "stuff" and had nothing more to work on. Unfortunately for both of them, Peter believed this.

One day, Peter went to their counselor for a session without Amy. He explained something that had happened a few days prior.

Earlier that year, Amy and Peter had attended a marriage conference which they both found extremely helpful. On the way home, Peter had asked Amy, "Would you be okay if we reviewed this

THE EPIDEMIC OF PASSIVITY: INTERNAL CONTRIBUTO..   49

material every few months and let each other know how we could better feel loved and respected?"

Amy agreed.

Several months later, Peter had approached Amy about reviewing their meeting book as discussed. He allowed her to go first, and for over an hour, he listened to Amy rail on him about how he was a lousy husband, how he doesn't show her love appropriately, how she feels so alone, and how he is the source of all her ill feelings.

Peter sat there patiently, listened intently, and made notes on how he could improve. When Amy was done, she got up to leave. Peter reminded her that he hadn't gone yet.

Amy replied, "Oh, God told me I'm doing everything I need for you and that I don't need to improve as a wife in any way, so we're done here."

With a devastated and crushed heart, Peter explained all this to his counselor.

His counselor, with a look of great compassion, asked, "Peter, why did you allow her to spew all of that at you for over an hour?"

The question stunned Peter because he didn't think he had an option. He replied, "Because I was picking up my cross."

The counselor replied, "That's not picking up your cross. It seems to me that you were trying to avoid conflict. Picking up your cross is doing what God tells you to do, even if the outcome isn't pleasant."

Those words rocked Peter's world.

The counselor then gave Peter a Bible and had him read Proverbs 4:23, "Above all else, guard your heart, for it is the wellspring of life."

Peter realized that he hadn't been guarding his heart. The verse read, "Above all else..." In other words, there's nothing more important than that. He had some things to ponder.

Over the next couple of months, Peter remained in his rut of doing everything he could to please Amy. However, seeing that his efforts only seemed to make things worse was becoming more and more disturbing to him. Then he had an epiphany.

While sitting with God one day, he remembered the words of

Jesus, "Love your neighbor as yourself." (Matthew 22:39) He pondered this for several minutes, and then it hit him.

Because he'd been allowing Amy to spew anything she wanted at him—and because he'd received it—he was not only *not* guarding his heart; he was also *not* showing love to himself.

Jesus said that we can only love others as we love ourselves.

PETER REALIZED THAT HIS DEPTH OF LOVING AMY COULD BE NO
GREATER THAN THE DEPTH TO WHICH HE LOVED HIMSELF.

This was a game-changer for Peter. For the first time, he saw that he at least had control over himself, and he no longer felt stuck in a game he couldn't win. As a result, he began to make changes. On the surface these didn't seem to help his relationship with Amy, but he felt more like a God-honoring man than ever before and had some renewed hope for his marriage.

He also realized that many well-intentioned Christians had previously given him unsound advice. They had said the Bible can be summarized in four words: "Love God. Love people."

He now saw that the truth was, "The Bible can be summarized in six words, 'Love God. Love yourself. Love people.' *In that order.*"

Peter began to develop strategies—similar to those we will discuss in the coming pages—to guard himself when he felt Amy was attempting to harm him. Amy reacted with anger each time he did this, but Peter experienced more and more peace knowing that he was now loving himself which allowed him to truly love Amy.

LOVE GOD.
LOVE YOURSELF.
LOVE PEOPLE.

If my wife is upset with me, God is too (Johnny & Sierra)

Bob, Johnny's mentor, started their lunch meeting together in an unusual way, "Johnny, I think it's time for you to fight for your marriage."

Surprised, Johnny said, "I thought that's what I've been doing."

Bob said, "I think it's time you confront Sierra (Johnny's wife) about her emotional affair with Curtis."

As Johnny took this in, a pit formed in his stomach. This had been going on for 10 years. Johnny hadn't labeled it as an "emotional affair," but he knew it was true. His fear of rejection had kept him from admitting the truth.

Sierra worked in the same office as Curtis, and they had become friends. Sierra often went to his house for parties and cookouts and sometimes invited Johnny to come too. He went along a couple of times but always felt extremely awkward and uncomfortable.

Other times, Curtis would call and talk with Sierra for long periods of time—while Sierra was sitting with Johnny. He even called once while Johnny and Sierra were on vacation, and Sierra walked along the beach for an hour talking with Curtis. Johnny often heard Sierra end their conversations by saying, "I love you too."

The thought of it made Johnny cringe and hurt him deeply. He knew her relationship with Curtis was wrong.

After several years she also began going over to Curtis's house to "visit with him" and watch television.

Several times, he'd told Sierra that he'd feel more comfortable if she didn't go to Curtis's house when she wasn't working. Sierra would curse at him and often storm out of the room. Johnny quickly learned that this topic was off-limits.

In recent years Sierra had occasionally told Johnny, "I wish you would open up. I feel closer to Curtis than I do you."

Upon hearing this, Johnny felt so disrespected and unloved. Throughout the years, he hesitated to bring it up; he thought his marriage might end if he did because Sierra's tie to Curtis was so strong.

And now, because of Bob's challenge, he knew he needed to enter into that conversation again. Besides, if Sierra was unhappy with him,

God would be unhappy with him also. After all, he needed to make her happy, right?

He thought that hiding his pain and remaining silent was showing love to Sierra. Like Peter in the previous story, he was not showing love to himself.

Johnny eventually confronted Sierra and shared his feelings. As expected, this did not go well and Sierra didn't talk to him for several days. However, for the first time in a long time, he experienced a level of peace which felt incredible to him.

Five months later, Sierra finally agreed to break off her relationship with Curtis and seek counseling to begin rebuilding their marriage.

Love means making her happy and never saying "no" (Tim & Sally)

Tim loved Sally. They'd been married seven years, and Tim felt that his primary role was to make Sally happy. To him, this was the evidence that he was a godly husband.

Tim's not sure where this false belief originated, but he remembered being at a huge men's event in a stadium and hearing the leader of the ministry say, "You can tell the depth of a man's walk with God by looking at the countenance of his wife's face."

This resonated with Tim and reinforced a lot of what he had read in marriage books. And because he was a goal-oriented guy, it gave him something to shoot for—to make Sally happy.

Without realizing it, Tim fell for the lie that he wasn't a man of God unless his wife was happy.

As a result, like Peter, Tim became codependent, walked on eggshells, never said "No," and allowed Sally to treat him poorly. Though other close friends of theirs could see this clearly, Tim remained blind to it.

Because Sally seemed to always want more and more of his time, Tim would give up healthy activities to make Sally happy. He thought,

If I just spend more time with her, then she'll treat me with the respect and affection I desire.

Tim was a business owner, and sometimes he needed to work longer hours to keep up. Since he was a "doer," he didn't mind it. He loved getting things done. It brought him peace because he experienced great anxiety when he had things left on his to-do list.

However, over time, he began to work shorter hours because he'd learned that his number one ministry was to his wife, and Tim wanted to honor God. He still got most of his tasks done, but he really had to hustle to make it happen. Tim became exhausted and all of this created more stress in his life.

Despite all his effort, things seemed to get worse, not better. It wasn't until years later that Tim realized he could never do enough to please Sally.

One time, a friend asked him, "If someone spits on you, does that make you mad?"

"Absolutely!"

"No, it doesn't. It makes you wet. It's your choice to be angry or not. *Happy wife, happy life* sounds true—and based on experience, sometimes it is. However, it's a deception. The implication is that we —as husbands—are responsible for our wives' happiness. But she is the only one responsible for her happiness. You're responsible *to* her but not *for* her.

His friend continued, "I began to free myself from passivity and timidity in my marriage when this truth finally settled in my heart four years ago."

In that moment, Tim realized that it was Sally's choice to be happy or not. Her happiness wasn't dependent upon him. Sure, he knew he shouldn't be a jerk—but recognizing the lie of being responsible for his wife's happiness freed him from slavery to Sally's emotions.

Tim began to play golf again once per week with his friends. He also stopped feeling guilty when he had to work a little longer in order to meet a deadline. Sally didn't respond well at first to these changes, but Tim began to feel freer—and more like the man he was designed to be.

I can fix this if I just try harder (Steve & Mary)

Steve had experienced many of the same issues as Peter and Tim. He, too, felt he just needed to do more and try harder.

One day, his counselor said, "Steve, I have an assignment for you. For the next six weeks, I want you to fast from (i.e. stop) caring about Mary."

Steve was flabbergasted. It made no sense to him but he was determined to try something new. But for the next week, he just couldn't get it. It totally went against what he believed he needed to do.

Then, begrudgingly, he gave it a try. It seemed strange at first, but he began to feel a great sense of freedom. Soon after, Steve realized how much he'd been a slave to Mary's demands. He was amazed.

After a couple weeks, Mary said to Steve, "Is everything okay? It seems like you're not spending much time with me."

Steve simply replied, "Everything's great. I'm just taking some time to work on me. Thanks for asking."

At the end of the six weeks, Steve didn't feel any closer to Mary but he never felt freer. He realized how much he needed to be in this healthier place so that he and Mary could begin to address their issues together.

In many instances, greater effort does produce greater results. However, in situations like Peter's, Tim's, and Steve's, more effort typically has the opposite effect. It can reinforce wives' unhealthy behaviors and attitudes—and your own too—enabling her to remain in those destructive practices.

WE CANNOT CHANGE
ANYONE OTHER THAN OURSELVES.

This is especially true when talking about our wives. Though we love our wives, we cannot change them.

God loves everyone, yet look at how many people never change. God can't make people change. Sure, His power enables transformation, but we must partner with Him in the change process.

The same is true of your wife. The best course of action is to guard your heart and to focus on your own growth path (keeping your side of the street clean).

Another lie that men believe deals with the quality of their effort on behalf of their marriages rather than on the quantity:

If I do it more rightly, or more perfectly, then things will change (Jack & Lucy)

Jack and Lucy had been married for 17 years. Jack regularly checked in with Lucy to ask, "How're you doing?"

One day Lucy told Jack, "I don't like the way you ask me that. It makes me feel like you think something's wrong with me. Say it another way next time."

Jack took her words to heart. He was reading a marriage book and discovered a new phrase. A few days later, he asked, "How's your love tank? Is it full or does it need filling?"

Lucy said, "I really like that!"

Jack was elated. He'd found the perfect phrase and had struck relational gold—until a month later when Lucy said, "I don't like that anymore. Say it a different way."

Many of us have been in Jack's shoes. *If I can only do it right next time then it'll be different.*

Many of us have come to realize that we cannot ever fully do it right. Face it: in some relationships you'll never be able to, no matter how hard you try.

YOU ARE NOT RESPONSIBLE FOR YOUR WIFE'S EMOTIONS,
AND YOU'RE NOT RESPONSIBLE FOR HER HAPPINESS.

The sooner we realize that we can't force our wives to change, or always do what she needs, or always do it "right." and instead stop trying to please our wives in this unhealthy way, the faster we find our way to freedom.

And understanding that you are not the one always at fault is critical as well.

It must be my fault

This lie shows up in all of the above stories. It's so easy as a man to think that it's our fault. Culture, the Church, others around us, and our false beliefs all steer us headlong into this lie.

It's honorable, responsible, and shows great humility to be open to discovering your issues and to want to fix them. However, it's not so honorable to take things upon yourself and beat yourself up over things that aren't your fault.

THE FACT IS THAT YOU ARE RESPONSIBLE
TO OTHERS BUT NOT *FOR* OTHERS.

It's your responsibility to treat your wife the way you would like to be treated. Is your wife treating you the way you'd like to be treated? If not, chances are you're living in a destructive environment, and this is a signal that *you* need to change (remember, you cannot change her).

For those of us in relationships where we find ourselves being passive, a better question may be, "Are you treating yourself as well as you treat others?" Remember, we can only love others to the depth that we love ourselves according to Jesus (see Matthew 22:39, Mark 12:31, and Luke 10:27).

My friend Ford Taylor says, "We do love our neighbors as we love ourselves and that's a problem—because we don't love ourselves much!"

I'm stuck, and I'm powerless (Carl & Shelly)

Carl and Shelly had been married for nearly 35 years. In that time, Carl had begun to realize the things that Peter, Tim, and Jack had learned. As he began to change his behaviors, things got very unpleasant with Shelly.

Specifically, she became extremely mean. These are some of the tamer things she said:

- "You're from Satan!"
- "You prideful bastard!"
- "Why don't you go crawl under that rock you came from?"

Carl had never heard such things from his wife before and began to wonder if he'd made a mistake in how he'd changed his behavior and began setting boundaries.

Then he met with a couple of his mentors. Sharing his concerns, he feared that Shelly might divorce him. They consoled him and gently brought him back to his mission of becoming a God-honoring husband.

They praised him for the work he'd done and the courage he'd exhibited. They told him that in order to honor God, he would need to walk in obedience to what God said rather than what most others, including Shelly, expressed.

They reminded him that it takes courage to follow God's will and to leave the outcomes to Him. They further encouraged Carl that by taking a stand, he was giving himself a shot at having the marriage that he, and God, desired.

Carl had come to learn several freeing truths. He wasn't stuck. He had power to change, and that gave him hope. However, he did *not* have the power to change Shelly.

Unfortunately, Shelly would not accept the "new" Carl and, after 11 months, filed for divorce. Though devastated, Carl was thankful for what God had revealed to him and what He was doing in him.

If I share what's happening with someone, they won't believe me, or they'll think I'm weak

This mentality is very understandable because of how culture views us as men and because of the insecurities some of us harbor. However, this is absolutely not true.

Certainly, sharing sensitive information with unhealthy people could lead to an unpleasant reaction (critical, non-compassionate, etc.). But sharing with Godly, safe people will more likely result in a positive and encouraging result.

In the story above, Carl received help from his mentors. In addition to mentors, others may find it in close friends and counselors.

Think about these questions when searching for safe people:

- Do they want what's best for me?
- Are they rooting for me to succeed? If I sense any jealousy or competition, I won't share at the same level I would share with safe others.
- Are they spiritually mature? I want them to be further along in their faith than I am or seeking God with the same or greater intensity than I do.
- Are they emotionally mature? I don't want someone who'll be critical, judgmental, or feel that they're there to give me advice all the time (legalistically trying to get me to accept all their viewpoints).
- Are they secure enough to challenge me when I need to be challenged? Will they speak hard truths to me?
- Are they trustworthy? Can I be certain that everything I share would never leave the room?

These people seldom just come up to us to offer help. It's up to us to find them. Ask God to reveal these people to you, and then be bold and ask if they'd fill this role (of helping you in your growth journey). I'll share more about the importance of this in Chapter 9.

Unconditional love means unconditional relationship (Jason & Cassandra)

Jason and Cassandra had been married for 11 years when Jason began to notice the decline in their relationship. This started about the time their fourth child was born. At that point, the level of stress level in their home mushroomed.

Cassandra dealt with this stress by calling Jason nasty names and continually criticizing him. Jason pleaded with Cassandra to see a counselor, but she refused, saying their issues were all his.

Dejected, Jason contacted a Christian counselor who came highly recommended by some trusted friends. On his first visit, he shared a snapshot of their home life and how he was trying to love Cassandra out of this rut.

Jason also shared that Cassandra demanded that he trust her explicitly. She believed that forgiveness meant the same thing as trust.

With compassion, his counselor said, "I know how much this has to hurt. I'm so sorry you're going through this. First, let's address the forgiveness piece. Forgiveness doesn't equal trust. Forgiveness cannot be earned, it is freely given.

"However, trust is to be given to those who are trustworthy. It sounds like you cannot trust Cassandra right now. Certainly, you can forgive her and should do so since unforgiveness only hurts you. However, forgiving her does not mean you need to trust her since she has shown herself untrustworthy."

At first, Jason felt a degree of relief. He wasn't crazy after all. Then the counselor said something that shocked Jason through and through:

"Jason, I respect your desire to unconditionally love Cassandra. However, unconditional love does not mean you need to give unconditional relationship."

Jason questioned that statement, and his counselor had him look at some Bible verses. The first was...

Better to live on a corner of the roof than share a house with a quarrelsome wife.
   ~*Proverbs 25:24*

Then Jason's counselor took him to passages in Scripture where God had set His own boundaries with his bride, Israel. Because of her poor behavior, God removed His presence from her (see Jeremiah 3:8, Isaiah 50:1, Ezekiel 21, Hosea 2).

Jason couldn't believe he'd missed this concept all these years. With his counselor's help, he put together a plan to set some boundaries. Chief among them was the following tactic: when Cassandra crossed the line, he would calmly say, "Cassandra, I'm no longer going to allow this. I need to remove myself until you can treat me in a more respectful way."

Though Cassandra did not appreciate this at first, this change provided some sanity for Jason and gave them a much better chance to enjoy a healthier marriage.

Why Men have Distorted Views

The reason men believe lies and become insecure boils down to two key contributors, and they're both related: fear (most often the fear of rejection) and the negative spiritual influence of our enemy.

In most, if not all, cases, these fears and negative spiritual influences find entry into our lives from earlier wounds that have become a stronghold. Strongholds are mentioned throughout Scripture and are defined as "a place that has been fortified so as to protect it against attack."[2]

Our wounds inspire us to build strongholds around places in our hearts to protect against similar attacks. Then these strongholds cause us to view life through a faulty filter which often leads us to be intimidated (timidity).

In the upcoming chapters, we'll walk through some things you can do, with God's help, to demolish these strongholds and free yourself.

But before we do that, let's examine how your current struggle is actually good news.

[6]

JESUS WAS A LOUSY MARKETER

A Counselor's Wisdom (Phil & Elise)

Phil had been seeing his counselor for the past four years. Initially, Phil's wife Elise had attended the counseling sessions with him, but 11 months ago, she'd told Phil that all of their issues were his fault.

Phil had believed that until a few weeks prior.

As hopeless as he'd ever been, Phil poured his heart out to his counselor.

"I feel stuck," he said. "I feel like I have no power to change anything, and I can't see a way out."

From his perspective, the rest of his life was going to be filled with pain, loneliness, and misery. He felt that nothing good could come of all this.

If you've ever been in a similar place, you know how depressing and lonely it is.

Scripture tells us that we are transformed by the renewing of our minds (see Romans 12:2). How can we renew our minds—how can we view our difficulty differently—so that we, too, can be transformed?

Jesus the Marketer?

A number of years ago my son and I began eating a Paleo-type diet where we eliminated all sugar and grains. Since we both loved ice cream, I decided to search the internet for Paleo ice cream recipes. Surprisingly I found a bunch.

I chose one that looked good and dug out our electric ice cream maker. It was about five years old but since we had only used it about six times, it still looked brand new.

Per the recipe, I put the ingredients in the canister. I added ice and then salt to the bucket; with great anticipation we turned it on, only to hear nothing!

Though the company touted that their product was durable and should last for years, my ice cream maker was dead. And I had only used it a handful of times! I was so disappointed!

Have you ever bought a product that didn't live up to the hype in its advertisement? Wouldn't it be refreshing if the marketing would include the drawbacks to the product so you could make an informed decision?

The problem with that approach is that stating the product's problems in an advertisement would be considered lousy marketing.

How did Jesus market what He came to bring us?

Consider some of these things He said to those who were considering following Him:

If anyone comes to me and does not hate his father and mother, his wife and children, his brothers and sisters—yes, even his own life—he cannot be my disciple. And anyone who does not carry his cross and follow me cannot be my disciple.
  ~Luke 14:26-27

In the same way, any of you who does not give up everything he has cannot be my disciple.
  ~Luke 14:33

And what about this passage?

When Jesus saw the crowd around him, he gave orders to cross to the other side of the lake. Then a teacher of the law came to him and said, "Teacher, I will follow you wherever you go."

Jesus replied, "Foxes have holes and birds of the air have nests, but the Son of Man has no place to lay his head."

Another disciple said to him, "Lord, first let me go and bury my father."

But Jesus told him, "Follow me, and let the dead bury their own dead."

~Matthew 8:18–22

Does that sound like someone trying to "sell" people on following Him?

In Luke 14:28–30 Jesus said this,

"Suppose one of you wants to build a tower. Will he not first sit down and estimate the cost to see if he has enough money to complete it?"

He was telling us that we must count the cost. In other words, following Him will cost us.

DO YOU WANT TO FOLLOW
JESUS OR NOT?

Clearly, Jesus wasn't interested in numbers. He wanted fully devoted followers instead.

If Jesus was a marketer, these might've been some of His slogans:

- Follow me, and you might be homeless (you won't have any place to lay your head.)
- Follow me, and you may make enemies out of your entire family.
- Give me everything you have, then you can follow me.

Obviously, Jesus also shared the innumerable and eternal benefits of following Him. But there's no denying it: *Jesus would make a lousy marketer...* at least from how we view marketing today. He certainly didn't sugarcoat things.

But what do we often do as followers of Jesus? Don't we sometimes try to "market" Him (or make Him sound really good) as if we're trying to get people "into" the club? "Say this prayer, and your life will be great!"

I contend that authentically following Jesus is a much more difficult road than not following Him. Jesus actually calls it a narrow road which leads to life; it's more difficult.

At the same time, it's also the most fulfilling road, and He promises to be there with you and to help you. But it's anything but easy. Billy Graham once said,

"TRUE FAITH AND SUFFERING FREQUENTLY GO HAND IN HAND. LIVING FOR CHRIST, WALKING IN HIS WAY, WILL NOT BE AN EASY PATH."

Ah, suffering. We haven't even touched on that yet.

*For you have been granted [the privilege] for Christ's sake not only to believe in (adhere to, rely on, and trust in) Him, **but also to suffer in His behalf.***
   ~Philippians 1:29 AMP, emphasis added

*To this you were called, because Christ suffered for you, leaving you an example, that **you should follow in his steps.***
   ~1 Peter 2:21, emphasis added

*Now if we are children, then we are heirs—heirs of God and co-heirs with Christ, **if indeed we share in his sufferings** in order that we may also share in his glory.*
   ~Romans 8:17 emphasis added

Did you know that, as followers of Jesus, we're called to share in

His sufferings? It's true, and many more verses in the Bible back this up.

Check out what 1 Peter 4:12–13 says:

*"Dear friends, **do not be surprised** at the painful trial you are suffering, as though something strange were happening to you. **But rejoice that you participate in the sufferings of Christ**, so that you may be overjoyed when his glory is revealed."* (emphasis added)

And Romans 8:17 says:

*Now if we are children, then we are heirs—heirs of God and co-heirs with Christ, **if indeed we share in his sufferings** in order that we may also share in his glory.* (emphasis added)

I've read this verse many times, yet it's amazing to me that when I face a trial, or suffering, I'm usually surprised. Many of us continually look for ways to make our lives more comfortable. As such, it's easy for us to be deceived into thinking that our lives should be pain-free.

The verse above says we should *expect* to suffer. It also says that we are to rejoice in our suffering. How is this possible?

Understanding that there is a purpose to our suffering is a key that can help us to rejoice even amid our darkest times.

Before proceeding, let me stop to assure you that I am in no way trying to minimize the pain you may be experiencing. I know how gut-wrenching it can be when your marriage is in disarray, especially when no one around you seems to understand.

I know how much pain you're in. I really do because I've been there. What I'm about to say is designed to bring a glimmer of hope into your darkness... I'm absolutely certain some good will come of it.

The Purpose to Your Pain

Let's look at what God's Word says about our pain and suffering and see if we can glean any benefits, or purpose, behind it:

To learn obedience

> *Although he was a son, he learned obedience from what he suffered.*
>   *~Hebrews 5:8*

If the King of kings needed to learn obedience, certainly we will too. Thus, suffering is required so that we, too, can learn obedience.

To humble and test us

> *Remember how the Lord your God led you all the way in the desert these forty years, to humble you and to test you in order to know what was in your heart, whether or not you would keep His commands.*
>   *~Deuteronomy 8:2*

Sometimes God leads us into the desert to humble us and to test us. It's fairly easy to see how humility is beneficial for us, but what about testing?

The Lord tests us to reveal to us what's in our hearts. (He already knows.) When we see it, we can choose to repent and receive His healing. Again, a very good thing for us.

So that we can comfort others

> "Praise be to the God and Father of our Lord Jesus Christ, the Father of compassion and the God of all comfort, who comforts us in all our troubles, so that we can comfort those in any trouble with the comfort we ourselves have received from God."
>   *~2 Corinthians 1:3-4*

Our suffering will help us to comfort others. Billy Graham said,

"Our sufferings may be hard to bear, but they teach us lessons which, in turn, equip and enable us to help others."

To produce perseverance, character and to give us hope

Not only so, but we also rejoice in our sufferings, because we know that suffering produces perseverance; perseverance, character; and character, hope.
  ~Romans 5:3–4

Our sufferings produce perseverance, help to develop our character, and give us hope.

To increase our faith and prove it genuine

In this you greatly rejoice, though now for a little while you may have had to suffer grief in all kinds of trials. These have come so that your faith—of greater worth than gold, which perishes even though refined by fire—may be proved genuine and may result in praise, glory and honor when Jesus Christ is revealed.
  ~1 Peter 1:6–7

God uses our suffering to increase our faith. Gold is refined in the fire, as is our faith.

To strengthen us

And the God of all grace, who called you to his eternal glory in Christ, after you have suffered a little while, will himself restore you and make you strong, firm and steadfast.
  ~1 Peter 5:10

God will restore us after we have suffered a little while, and He will make us strong, firm and steadfast.

To keep us from becoming conceited

To keep me from becoming conceited because of these surpassingly great revelations, there was given me a thorn in my flesh, a messenger of Satan, to torment me.
~2 Corinthians 12:7

Pain and suffering helps us be less conceited... that is, more humble.

To develop our perseverance

Consider it pure joy, my brothers, whenever you face trials of many kinds, because you know that the testing of your faith develops perseverance. Perseverance must finish its work so that you may be mature and complete, not lacking anything.
~James 1:2–4

Our suffering helps us develop perseverance which helps us to be more mature and complete.

To help us know and rely on God more

We do not want you to be uninformed, brothers, about the hardships we suffered in the province of Asia. We were under great pressure, far beyond our ability to endure, so that we despaired even of life. Indeed, in our hearts we felt the sentence of death. But this happened that we might not rely on ourselves but on God, who raises the dead.
~2 Corinthians 1:8–9

Our sufferings also help us to know and rely on God more. This may be the most valuable benefit to us.

UNFORTUNATELY, PROSPERITY SELDOM, IF EVER,
PRODUCES CHARACTER IN US OR HELPS US TO GROW.

Whose Idea is This?

My son Robert, like most of us, really likes his comfort zone. From a very early age, he hasn't liked trying anything new (until recently).

This included trying new foods when he was very young. I estimate that more than 95 percent of the time, when he would try a new food, he'd give a sheepish grin and say something like, "I *do* like it."

The same is true with activities. Because he favored routine and because of some negative experiences on the baseball diamond and the basketball court, he was content to stay inside and watch TV or play video games… that was his comfort zone.

In his early teen years, I told Robert that I wanted him doing something physical. He said, "There's nothing to do that I like."

I recognized that what he was really saying was, "I don't want to try anything new. I'm happy right here."

Several people suggested he try martial arts, so I arranged to have him do a trial run. On the way to the facility, he was extremely agitated with me and told me he was sure he would hate it. When we arrived, he was so mad that he wouldn't even look the instructor in the eyes.

The instructor suggested Robert and I do a little sparring, and he put us through the paces. Though we had no clue about what we were doing, I could tell Robert was enjoying it.

Afterward he asked Robert what he thought, and he responded, "It was okay… at least it was better than I thought it was going to be."

What he was really saying was, "I loved it, but I can't say that because I thought I would hate it."

For three and a half years, I drove him to classes twice a week. Because the sessions were physically and mentally demanding, he often wouldn't want to go. However, immediately afterward he would tell me he was so glad that he went.

He grew tremendously during this time, and three and a half years later he tested and received his black belt. I'm so proud of him for staying the course and going through the painful process.

Years after this experience, Robert told me, "I'm so thankful that you pushed me into karate. I've realized how that taught me the value of discipline and the value of a structured routine. I never thought a black belt was a possibility for me, but it showed me how taking one step after another and being persistent can get you to places you never dreamed of being."

In this case, it took me, his dad, to push him into this. If left to himself, Robert would've remained at home in his comfort zone. This is often what happens to us in many areas of our lives, not the least of which is in our marriages.

We become desensitized to the behavior of our wives and to our own passivity. We normalize our roles and behaviors and sit comfortably in deterioration and destruction... like the proverbial frog in the kettle of water slowly coming to a boil.

I love my son so much that I was willing to push him into this "pain" so that he could grow into a better version of himself. The same is true with our Heavenly Dad and us. He allows us to experience pain, trouble, and chaos because He loves us so much and He knows how it will help us.

What you're presently experiencing in your marriage is not an exception. Though it may not feel like it, God *is* using this for good in your life (see Romans 8:28).

> "SMOOTH SEAS DON'T MAKE SKILLFUL SAILORS."
> ~ AFRICAN PROVERB

As mentioned in Chapter 2, the past 10-15 years have been,

without question, the most painful time of my life. However, this decade has also brought me the most growth and fulfillment I've ever experienced.

Now on the other side of that tumultuous time, I feel extremely blessed. I'm grateful for what I'm doing, who I'm becoming, and for the amazing people in my life. Dad (God) knew how to choose better for me than I could choose for myself.

Does the pain still hurt? Absolutely! But as I look over the landscape of my life, I see more clearly how God is using it to shape me and guide me.

My point in all of this is to remind you that there is great purpose in your pain. Though I understand you may not be able to see it (there are still some days when I can't see it), I promise God wants to bring great purpose into your life.

Phil & Elise Revisited

At the beginning of this chapter we learned about Phil and Elise and Phil feeling as if he were stuck and that nothing good could come from his marital situation.

After seeing his counselor for several months—without Elise—Phil began to see progress in how he was viewing his situation. He blamed Elise for their discord much less and he was owning his part of the conflict. This gave him hope because he could do something about his side of the street.

Phil was amazed because he saw for the first time how God was using his painful situation as a catalyst for growth in himself.

Refining

God wants to bring His Kingdom, as it is in Heaven, to Earth. And He has selected you and me to help Him do it. In order for Him to fulfill this through us, He must refine us. This refining is typically done in the furnace of suffering.

When we can fully grasp that, we can approach difficulty differently.

When we're faced with difficulty, our default question tends to be, "God, why is this happening to me?" If we can change that question, we can begin to be transformed (see Romans 12:2). The quicker we can turn to the Lord and say, "Okay God...

- what's the purpose of this?"
- what are you teaching me?"
- what do you have for me in this?"

... then the quicker we can actually rejoice in our suffering.

CS Lewis once said,

"If you look for truth, you may find comfort in the end; if you look for comfort you will not get either comfort or truth, only soft soap and wishful thinking to begin, and in the end, despair."

So we really have two choices:

1. To seek after truth, which means seeking Jesus—with no guarantee of comfort, or:
2. To seek after comfort and in the end find only despair.

Will you join me in seeking after Truth? If so, let's continue and discover some practical steps you can take to free yourself from the prison of passivity and timidity.

MARCHING ORDERS

Two Impossible Choices

I f you're like many Christian men in difficult marriages, you might be thinking that you have only two choices: 1) suck it up and continue being a doormat or, 2) leave your wife.

This thinking keeps men stuck in despair since neither option is appealing. The thought of treading water feels like a prison sentence. And divorce sounds terribly painful, and it impacts many more people than just you and your wife.

However, another way can bring you freedom and joy and could quite possibly help to rebuild your marriage into the beautiful union that God desires for you.

In the books of 1st and 2nd Timothy, Paul writes to his young protégé to give him his marching orders. In his first letter, Paul tells Timothy, "Don't let anyone look down on you because you are young, but set an example for the believers in speech, in life, in love, in faith and in purity." (1 Timothy 4:12)

In his second letter, Paul writes, "For this reason I remind you to fan into flame the gift of God, which is in you through the laying on of my hands. For God did not give us a spirit of timidity, but a spirit of power, of love and of self-discipline." (2 Timothy 1:6–7)

In much the same way, I'm giving you your marching orders, a plan for you to follow. Let's briefly unpack these verses and see how they apply to you:

Don't let anyone look down on you because you are young

Being young is not only a function of one's age but can also apply to our experience level. Though I was an adult, I was young when it came to understanding and carrying out my godly role as a husband.

The fact is, we don't know what we don't know. This isn't our fault, unless we purposely kept ourselves from seeking wisdom and understanding. So don't let anyone (including your wife) look down on you because you are "young."

And because you've read this far, you've learned some things that have probably surprised you. When you begin to put these into practice, you'll be showing wisdom. You're not as young as when you started this book—you're growing.

But set an example for the believers in speech, in life, in love, in faith and in purity.

Setting an example is critical for you. No matter what your past looks like, it's your role to walk in these instructions to the best of your ability... regardless of how you're treated!

A good friend of mine says that when we're in an unhealthy relationship, our job is to "be the straight line to the crooked." In other words, we're to lead by example. When we act appropriately, we shine a light on the other person's inappropriate behavior and, hopefully, we reveal to them a better way.

The difficulty in this is that, often the other person may not want to acknowledge their inappropriate behavior. As such, it can appear that they don't want to be aware—they don't want to be "in the light." They may even lash out at you or become more combative.

If this is the case, take heart; you're on the right track. You're successfully becoming a straight line to the crooked.

> **So set an example in your speech, in your life, in your faith, by remaining pure, and in the way you love. (Remember: love includes setting boundaries, speaking truth and loving yourself.)**

For this reason I remind you to fan into flame the gift of God, which is in you through the laying on of my hands.

Paul is reminding Timothy that he had previously anointed and imparted something into Timothy by laying hands upon him.

Paul mentored Timothy. I pray that, someday, you'll pass this message I'm giving you onto another man.

I'm imparting a message to you—or a gift—of freedom and hope. We'll be breaking off "spirits" (including the religious spirit) which have kept us bound for too long.

It's your responsibility to fan that gift into a flame. You can do that by seeking God and following the suggestions in this book that are appropriate for you.

For God did not give us a spirit of timidity, but a spirit of power, of love and of self-discipline.

Paul was reminding Timothy—and us—that timidity doesn't come from God. Satan used passivity with Adam back in the Garden of Eden as we discussed in Chapter 4. Adam's actions (or inaction) led to the first sin: Adam standing by, while his wife ate of the forbidden fruit. (His passivity and timidity *was* the first sin!)

God did not give us timidity, but instead He has given each of us power, love, self-discipline, and/or a sound mind (some translations use *a sound mind* instead of *self-discipline*).

It's time that you walk in the power and authority God has given you. But keep in mind that this does not give you permission to be a jerk or to abuse your wife. It's very easy to swing the pendulum too far when making changes in our lives, so be careful here. (We'll cover this more in Chapter 12.)

You must walk in the fullness of love, not just the bogus view of love that culture (and the Church, at times) tries to push on us. To review this idea, see Chapter 3 and Chapter 4.

Now is the time for us to walk in self-discipline and with a sound mind rather than acting out of our flesh by yelling back at our wives or behaving in any other ungodly ways.

IT'S TIME TO BE THE STRAIGHT LINE TO THE CROOKED.
IT'S YOUR JOB TO LEAD YOUR WIFE IN THIS WAY.

So I will add my voice to Paul's and exhort you...

DON'T BE TIMID!

Mighty Warrior

I want to acknowledge you. By reading to this point, you've shown that you're hungry for answers to your marital challenges.

Average guys wouldn't have done this. You have proven that you're not an average guy. In fact, you've proven that you're willing to fight for your freedom and for your marriage.

YOU, MY FRIEND,
ARE A MIGHTY WARRIOR.

Trust me—I get the fact that you may not be feeling like one. But you are.

Consider a young man named Gideon. The Midianites, a rival people group, would continually destroy his town's crops. He was so afraid of this enemy that he was hiding out and threshing wheat in a winepress to keep it away from Israel's enemies. In other words, not the best example of a mighty warrior. But...

All of a sudden, Gideon is visited by the angel of the Lord who says, "The LORD is with you, mighty warrior."

"But sir," Gideon replied, "if the LORD is with us, why has all this happened to us? Where are all his wonders that our fathers told us about when they said, 'Did not the LORD bring us up out of Egypt?' But now the LORD has abandoned us and put us into the hand of Midian."

The LORD turned to him and said, "Go in the strength you have and save Israel out of Midian's hand. Am I not sending you?"

"But Lord," Gideon asked, "how can I save Israel? My clan is the weakest in Manasseh, and I am the least in my family."

~Judges 6:12–15

This comforts me because I have too often felt and acted like Gideon in this passage. If you have too, it's time to lay that aside and be the mighty warrior God has called you to be!

To act as a warrior, it would be good to understand something about courage. John Maxwell says,

"Courage isn't an absence of fear. It's doing what you are afraid to do. It's having the power to let go of the familiar and forge ahead into new territory."

I would add that courage can also be defined as obeying God regardless of what the outcome might be.

Like Gideon, Joshua faced a formidable assignment.

God encouraged him with the following words:

After the death of Moses the servant of the LORD, the LORD said to Joshua son

of Nun, Moses' aide: "Moses my servant is dead. Now then, you and all these people, get ready to cross the Jordan River into the land I am about to give to them—to the Israelites.

I will give you every place where you set your foot, as I promised Moses. Your territory will extend from the desert to Lebanon, and from the great river, the Euphrates—all the Hittite country—to the Great Sea on the west.

No one will be able to stand up against you all the days of your life. As I was with Moses, so I will be with you; I will never leave you nor forsake you.

"Be strong and courageous, because you will lead these people to inherit the land I swore to their forefathers to give them. Be strong and very courageous.

Be careful to obey all the law my servant Moses gave you; do not turn from it to the right or to the left, that you may be successful wherever you go. Do not let this Book of the Law depart from your mouth; meditate on it day and night, so that you may be careful to do everything written in it.

Then you will be prosperous and successful. Have I not commanded you? Be strong and courageous. Do not be terrified; do not be discouraged, for the LORD your God will be with you wherever you go."

~Joshua 1:1–9

Please read that passage again and take note of the number of times God tells Joshua to be strong and courageous. He says those very words to you right now as well.

God says to you now,

"**BE STRONG AND COURAGEOUS, MY SON.
I AM WITH YOU.**"

And with this promise, let's begin to assemble our plan of action.

[8]
DISENGAGE

An Encouraging Friend (Joel & Emily)

Joel sat alone in his family room, head in his hands, sobbing. *What's happened to my marriage? Why am I in so much pain? And why can't I do anything about it?*

Joel and Emily had been married for 17 years, but throughout that time, their marriage had grown rockier and rockier. Now, Joel felt as though he couldn't even talk to her anymore.

The last time he'd tried—five minutes earlier—had ended with screaming and the bedroom door slamming in his face.

God, why is this happening? Why can't I make this better?

Click.

The bedroom door opened, and Joel's chest filled with a mix of hope and fear, both at once. A pillow came flying toward him and landed at his feet, and then the bedroom door slammed shut again.

Another night on the couch. What would that solve?

Emotion racked his body as he sighed and fought back his tears.

He stood, got himself a blanket from the hall closet, and made up the couch in the family room. He checked the time on the microwave.

The numerals "3:12" glowed in amber light next to a smaller "a.m." designation.

Joel shook his head. He couldn't keep doing this.

At least once a week, Joel and Emily spiraled into bitter feuds that started at 11:00pm or midnight and lasted for hours. Joel was already losing enough sleep over their marriage, and that was without staying up all hours of the night fighting with Emily. This had to stop.

Work was going to be rough tomorrow—or today, technically.

Exhausted and broken, Joel switched off the lights, flopped onto the couch, and closed his eyes.

The next morning, as soon as he woke up, Joel texted Max, the marriage counselor who'd been working with Joel and Emily. Joel asked if they could meet up, and while he was brushing his teeth in the guest bathroom, his phone dinged.

Max had invited him to his office downtown. He'd had a last-minute cancellation for a session around lunchtime and could fit Joel in. Joel confirmed with a reply text and hopped in the shower, still groggy from only two hours of sleep the night before.

When he got out of the shower, Emily was still in the bedroom with the door closed. Joel needed clothes for the day, so he knocked softly and turned the handle.

As he entered, Emily glared at him from the bed. She lay there in the dark, half-asleep.

"I just need to grab some clothes. Sorry."

Why am I apologizing? This isn't an unreasonable thing. Joel considered his apology. *Maybe it will help her be less angry.*

He'd certainly have a lot more apologizing to do later, based on the aftermath of his previous all-night fights with Emily.

Joel grabbed what he needed and shut the door behind him.

Joel trudged through the workday, surviving with only sheer determination and extra caffeine. When lunchtime finally rolled around, Joel's heart pounded faster in anticipation of his meeting, but he reassured himself that meeting with Max would help.

It has to.

When Joel walked into Max's office, Max welcomed him and shook his hand.

"Good to see you again, Joel."

"Likewise, Max."

They sat down on the plush chairs in Max's office and exchanged pleasantries for a few minutes just to catch up, and then Max promptly shifted the conversation.

"So how are things with Emily?"

Joel admired Max's straight-to-the-point approach. It had helped delve into the heart of many issues between Joel and Emily during their counseling sessions.

"Not good," Joel replied. "Things have gotten worse since we stopped coming to see you together."

A few months back, Emily had made the decision that she was done with counseling. At the time, she'd said, *"God told me that I don't need to go to counseling anymore since all of our issues are because of you. You need to get healed. You're very unhealthy."*

Those words had cut Joel to his core and left him feeling more alone than ever.

As Joel described his last several fights with Emily, Max listened intently. Joel concluded by saying, "I've scheduled romantic date nights and weekend getaways. I've spent more time with Emily and even left work early to do so. I've kept a tight rein on what I say to her, and I repeatedly emphasize my love and devotion to her.

"I pray more and more, for Emily and myself. I even started praying differently, asking God to reveal Himself to us both, to have His way in both of us, and for His will to be done. But it seems like no matter what I do, it just keeps getting worse."

When Joel finished, Max remained silent for a moment. He exhaled a long breath and leaned forward.

"Joel, you've been coming to me for counseling for five years," he began. "In that time, you've told me all the things you've done to try to fix your marriage. You've avoided confronting Emily. You've danced around sensitive issues with her. In all of that time, as you've just told me, things have mostly gotten worse. Correct?"

Joel nodded solemnly.

"A while back, you told me you're afraid that someday you'll get into a fight that will lead to a divorce, because of your parents' divorce."

Joel and Max had worked through this concept several years ago in a few one-on-one counseling sessions. Because Joel's parents had divorced, he worried the same thing would happen to him. He never remembered his parents arguing, and that had caused a couple of issues for him.

First, he'd never seen healthy conflict modeled. Second, he figured that if his parents got divorced without arguing, then an argument in his marriage would mean divorce was inevitable. Max had helped him better understand and address these concerns, but with how things had been going recently, Joel was second-guessing everything.

"And you've been tolerating Emily's abusive, demeaning treatment with the hope of avoiding a divorce," Max continued.

Joel nodded again.

"Your default mode is to move toward Emily, but that hasn't been working," Max said. "So what I want you to try now is to disengage."

Disengage? Joel stared at him. "What does that mean?"

"It means that you stop your continual pursuit and remove yourself from Emily's presence when she behaves contentiously toward you. Literally leave the room if you have to."

The idea stunned Joel. In fact, it seemed downright *un-Christian.* "I don't understand. Why do you think this will help?"

"The reality is that you've been ignoring your own needs to try to meet Emily's, and your own wellbeing has suffered as a result. If you're not healthy, how can you care for someone else? Disengaging is one way to reverse this."

Max's words baffled Joel, but the act of disengaging was one thing Joel hadn't tried yet. And Max had certainly helped them before—just never in a way like this.

Though incredulous, Joel decided to give it a shot. Max listed several situations in the Bible in which men received similar instructions, discussed them a bit with Joel, and encouraged Joel to look for more on his own.

With renewed optimism, Joel thanked Max, determined to give this new theory a try, and he headed out of the office with a measure of confidence and hope that he hadn't felt in a long time.

Several days had passed since Joel's meeting with Max. Joel was still skeptical about the concept of disengaging, so he decided to do as Max suggested and spend some time in the Bible to see if there were more instructions about disengaging.

Over the course of a couple of hours, he was shocked to find the following verses which instruct us to leave the presence of someone who is mistreating us (the behavior is in parenthesis):

- Proverbs 21:9; 21:19 25:4 (a contentious woman)
- Titus 3:10, Romans 16:17 (a divisive person)
- 2 Timothy 3:5 (those who are abusive, unholy, unforgiving, slanderous, without self-control, brutal, treacherous, lovers of pleasure, having a form of godliness but denying its power)
- Proverbs 9:12, 22:10; Psalm 1:1–4 (a scoffer or one who mocks)
- Matthew 10:14; Mark 6:11; Luke 10:11 (those who won't welcome you or listen to you)

- Ephesians 5:6–7 (those who excuse their sin or use empty words)
- Ephesians 5:11 (those who do evil deeds)
- 2 Thessalonians 3:6 (those who are idle)
- 1 Corinthians 5:5, 11–13 (those who are sexually immoral, greedy, practicing idolatry, revilers—which means those who use abusive language, verbal abuse, slander—drunkards, slanderous)
- 1 Corinthians 6:18 (those who are immoral)
- 1 Corinthians 10:14 (those who practice idolatry)
- Proverbs 13:20 + 14:7 (those who are fools—which means insolent, rebellious, arrogant, lacking understanding).[1]
- Proverbs 22:24–25 (those who are angry or easily angered)
- 2 John 9–10 (those who don't follow the teaching of Christ)
- Matthew 18 (one who sins against you and is not won over through the input of others)

In addition, he found some other verses that seemed to support Max's suggestion:

- Ezra 10:2–11 and Nehemiah 13:23–27 (don't allow unholy unions which cause a hindrance to your ministry)
- 1 Corinthians 15:13 (bad company ruins good morals)

And two verses really struck him. The first was:

Above all else, guard your heart, for it is the wellspring of life.
   ~Proverbs 4:23

He realized that by allowing Emily to treat him as she had been, he hadn't been "guarding his heart." He also saw that King Solomon had said to do this, "above all else" (see Proverbs 4:23). In other words, guarding our hearts is of the utmost importance because everything in life flows from our hearts.

The second verse that really hit him came from the book of Revelation where Jesus was speaking to the Church in Thyatira. Jesus is commending them for all the good they've done:

"I know your deeds, your love and faith, your service and perseverance, and that you are now doing more than you did at first."
   ~Revelation 2:19

He thought, *Wow, wouldn't it be great to have that said about me?* Then he read verse 20:

"Nevertheless, I have this against you: You tolerate that woman Jezebel who calls herself a prophetess."

Jesus then states that because she has misled others and she has not repented—though Jesus has given her time—*"... I will cast her on a bed of suffering and I will make those who commit adultery with her suffer intensely, unless they repent of her ways."*

Joel was stunned. He'd learned a bit about Jezebel over the years and, based on those teachings, had come to understand that Jezebel was a controlling, jealous, and manipulative spirit or principality. (The Jezebel in Revelation is named after King Ahab's wife.) He realized that he had been tolerating this type of behavior and wondered if he was, by extension, "tolerating Jezebel."

Whether the Jezebel spirit was involved or not, he'd determined to no longer tolerate Emily's negative and hurtful behavior.

But how could he do it? It seemed that every time he tried to break out of his passive ways, he'd find himself back there again. Seeing no way out, he began to seek God regularly about the answer to this question.

Joel then read the following passage in a book by Francis Frangipane that stopped him in his tracks:

If a husband is afraid of his strong-willed wife or unable to serve as the head of his household, although he is not in the worship building, he is still in the church tolerating Jezebel. Our time spent in the worship service is necessary, but it is a very small part of our continuing church-life. It is in the routine things of daily living where the strongholds of Jezebel must be confronted and destroyed.

To win against Jezebel, one must conquer the nature of Ahab.[2]

Joel realized that he was indeed "tolerating Jezebel" and saw how much it displeased the Lord. He realized with greater clarity that the issue was his.

He needed to conquer his "Ahab nature" (passivity and timidity) for his own sake, his wife's sake, and the sake of their marriage. Conquering "Ahab" would help bring healing to Emily—to conquer "Jezebel."

About this time, Joel found himself in a discussion with some trusted friends about some work-related issues. One comment really hit him: "What you tolerate will become standard practice."

He knew God was speaking to him about his penchant for passivity. He drove home that evening with renewed resolve to no longer tolerate Jezebel.

Over time, Joel began to remove himself when Emily acted contentiously around him. Though doing so was very foreign to him, and though Emily got furious when he did this, he began to feel freer and in greater control. And a glimmer of hope emerged on the horizon as he began to break free of the grips of Ahab.

Your Disengagement Strategy

Disengaging doesn't sound like a very manly thing to do; however, in cases like this, it is one of the most courageous things we can do.

Why? Because most wives of passive husbands desire to engage us in a battle of words. These are battles we cannot win. In most cases, we leave wounded and battered, wondering what went wrong.

Here is the simplest way to implement this. When your wife talks disrespectfully to you or acts contentiously, *calmly* say something like, "I'm sorry, but that sort of language (behavior, or whatever) makes me feel disrespected (or whatever you're feeling). I'm willing to continue this discussion when you can speak to me respectfully. Until then, I need to go to another room."

After disengaging, seek God to determine what you're feeling, and ask Him where those feelings are coming from. Ask Him what He wants to show you in this moment.

This is also a tremendous time to pray for God's healing for you and your wife. Though you may not feel like it, praying for her—and yourself—is, perhaps, the most productive thing you can do.

Your disengagement will probably make your wife extremely unhappy. In fact, she could become belligerent toward you.

Understand that when you step out of your comfort zone, that action automatically takes her out of *her* comfort zone as well. Since she's used to being in control, this will feel awkward, and she may react negatively.

Though it may feel terrible, this is a very positive sign because it indicates that change is occurring.

KEEP THE COURSE AND RESIST THE TEMPTATION TO CALM YOUR WIFE'S
STORM. YOU'LL BE TEMPTED TO MAKE THINGS RIGHT AGAIN,
BUT THAT'S WHAT GOT YOU IN THIS PLACE TO BEGIN WITH.

Remember, you're making a bold and courageous change that can pay tremendous dividends in you and your marriage.

[9]
YOUR LIFE-TEAM

"Choose someone whose way of life as well as words, and whose very
face as mirroring the character that lies behind it, have won your
approval. Be always pointing him out to yourself either as your
guardian or as your model. This is a need, in my view, for someone as
a standard against which our characters can measure themselves.
Without a ruler to do it against you won't make the crooked straight."
~Seneca, *Letters From a Stoic*

Joel recognized the importance of finding trusted advisers to
help him see truth amid his struggles, so he began building a
Life-Team—in addition to his counselor, Max—to help
guide him.

He realized that his faulty thinking had ushered him into this
place of misery in his marriage. He also realized that he couldn't trust
his thinking anymore because he wasn't sure which of the "truths" he
had believed were actually lies. He knew he needed others to help
guide him into the truth to replace the lies which had taken him off
course.

Several years ago, he'd reached out to Vince, a local pastor who was also a friend, and asked him to mentor him. So they were already getting together every two weeks.

Joel naturally asked Vince to be on the lookout for faulty thinking and to challenge him. He also became very vulnerable with Vince and shared everything that was going on in his marriage.

Joel also asked a friend from church to mentor him in his role as a husband. He had a marriage ministry and knew Joel and Emily well. Joel met with him every few weeks or whenever he needed input.

Emily didn't like Joel meeting with this mentor because he and his wife were friends of theirs. She felt it was inappropriate for him to be helping Joel since he knew them both so well.

In response, Joel suggested Emily ask his wife to meet with her as well which Emily dismissed. Despite Emily's protests, Joel felt strongly that this wise man could help him become more whole and that his familiarity with their situation would be an asset.

Joel also found several other pastors—including his own—from whom he could seek counsel along with some godly leaders he respected. Some of these were local, and others were out of state.

OVER THE NEXT SEVERAL YEARS, THIS LIFE-TEAM BECAME JOEL'S LIFELINE... SO MUCH SO THAT HE OFTEN WEPT WITH GRATITUDE FOR THEM.

After Joel received Max's instructions to disengage from Emily (at certain times), he met with several of his Life-Team members to process this with them. Doing so proved incredibly valuable because they affirmed that this was also what they sensed God saying. That wisdom emboldened Joel to follow through with this new set of actions that had initially seemed so uncomfortable and unnatural.

Though Joel felt extremely lonely in his home, his team also helped him to realize that he wasn't alone. They reminded him of a story in Exodus.

During a particular battle, as Moses held his arms up in the air, his troops were winning the battle. However, Moses' arms eventually grew tired and when he dropped them, his troops began to lose.

So Aaron and Hur came beside Moses and held his arms in the air, enabling them to win the battle (see Exodus 17:8–13). Joel so often felt that the amazing people on his Life-Team were his "Aaron and Hur."

Joel held two traits as paramount for his Life-Team: each member of his team had to be both trustworthy and a truth-teller. He knew he could count on them to be there for him, and they would keep everything confidential. They also weren't afraid to get in Joel's face and challenge him when he was off-base.

HIS LIFE-TEAM DIDN'T ALLOW HIM TO COMPLAIN ABOUT EMILY. WHENEVER HE TRIED TO MAKE IT ABOUT HER, THEY REDIRECTED IT BACK TO WHAT HE COULD CONTROL... HIMSELF.

Though he often wanted to make it about Emily, over time he grew thankful that his team wouldn't allow that. That mentality enabled him to more quickly work on changing himself.

The Lone Ranger

Many of us admire the Lone Ranger. You know, the guy who single-handedly swoops in to rescue the damsel in distress just before disaster strikes. The same could be said for Spiderman or many other super heroes. And as a result, some of us attempt to lead our lives in the same manner... by flying solo.

It's so easy to get stuck in the "going solo" track of life because...

- It feeds our egos and makes us feel important
- Many people think that seeking help indicates weakness
- Some men, especially those who are insecure, won't admit that they need help because they believe they'll need to turn in their "Man Card"

- It seems much easier to go it alone than asking others for help
- It avoids having to coordinate schedules, etc.

THE LONE RANGER EXCUSES ARE BUILT ON FAULTY THINKING AND LIES THAT LEAD TO A DARK SIDE OF MANHOOD.

Many men in difficult relationships isolate themselves—often for the reasons listed above. When things go sideways, we tend to detach from others until the storm passes. After all, asking for help seems so weak.

As much as some people don't want to admit it, we have a spiritual adversary who is real. Consider what Peter says in 1 Peter 5:8, "Be alert and of sober mind. Your enemy the devil prowls around like a roaring lion looking for someone to devour."

Think about how that verse plays out in nature. Have you ever watched a lion hunt a zebra on TV? If so, you probably know that the lion always goes after the zebra that's by itself.

In the verse mentioned, the word "devil" comes from the Greek word *diabolos*. And one of the meanings of *diabolos* is "to divide."[1]

ISOLATION LEADS TO US PLAYING RIGHT INTO OUR ENEMY'S HANDS.

Though we sometimes think that asking for help and rallying support appears weak, the truth is that it's a sign of great strength and humility—it takes emotional courage to be open with others and seek their assistance. Remember, even the Lone Ranger had Tonto by his side.

Here are some benefits of seeking help and gathering with others:

- **Encouragement:** Being a man is difficult today, and men often need encouragement to keep going. "Let us not give up meeting together, as some are in the habit of doing, but let us encourage one another—and all the more as you see the Day approaching." (Hebrews 10:25)

- **Correction:** Because of the pain you may be feeling, you might not want to hear the truth for fear of taking on more pain. However, what you need now more than ever is the truth. "Wounds from a friend can be trusted, but an enemy multiplies kisses." (Proverbs 27:6)

- **Growth:** A man can stand upright and be principled when others hold him accountable. "As iron sharpens iron, so one man sharpens another." (Proverbs 27:6)

- **Better Decision Making:** Strong men recognize that they don't have all the answers; they realize that their decision-making will improve when they surround themselves with wise counselors. "Plans fail for lack of counsel, but with many advisers, they succeed." (Proverbs 15:22)

- **Healing:** All men carry wounds that need healing. According to the Bible, healing takes place in a community. "Therefore confess your sins to each other and pray for each other so that you may be healed." (James 5:16)

- **Fulfillment:** As a man, you have great opportunity to speak into the lives of those around you, especially your wife and kids; this can bring great fulfillment. When we are open and looking for God to use us, we can make a significant difference in the lives of others. "Just as each of us has one body with many members, and these members do not all have the same function, so in Christ, we who are many forms one body, and each member belongs to all the others." (Romans 12:4–5)

- **Better Chance of Winning:** By tapping into the gifts and talents of others, your odds of succeeding as a leader are much greater. "For waging war, you need guidance and for victory, many advisers." (Proverbs 24:6)

- **It's Better, and it Makes Sense:** This is true, especially when you are hurting. Two are better than one because they have a good return for their work: "If one falls down, his friend can help him up. But pity the man who falls and has no one to help him up!" (Ecclesiastes 4:9–10)

I can attest to these truths firsthand. God has placed incredible people in my life and, though I have faced significant difficulty in my life, they have helped me to see so much good in all of it and find healing. I view these wonderful people as a tangible expression of God's immense love for me.

Though some of my difficulties continue, I remember that I have the support of my own Life-Team, and I feel more loved by God than ever before. This has enabled me to not only get through trials but to actually flourish in the midst of them.

Doubts

Joel's Doubts

Over the next several months, Joel questioned if he was doing the right thing. It still didn't *feel* natural or biblical. Was it possible his Life-Team was wrong in the counsel they were giving him?

As he wrestled with these questions, he asked God to reveal the truth. During such times, he often reflected on how he'd assembled his Life-Team, and he began to identify which of their qualities had helped give him confidence in their counsel:

- Many of them had extensive experience in dealing with relationship issues in their roles as pastors, counselors, or marriage ministry leaders.
- Even though passivity and timidity in men is not often discussed, each of the members of his team was adept at helping him navigate his issues.
- When necessary, the members of his Life-Team did not refrain from challenging Joel. In other words, they didn't

always agree with him which was a strong indicator that they were indeed true friends ("Wounds from a friend can be trusted, but an enemy multiplies kisses." Proverbs 27:6)

- He never met with them as an entire group, usually only individually and sometimes several at a time. So when they were all saying the same thing, he took notice. This made Joel think of Proverbs 11:14, "many advisers make victory sure."

Because of the support and encouragement from his Life-Team, Joel stayed the course; he was learning a new way of living. He had adopted a healthier process of thinking and dug deeper into his Biblical understanding.

Unfortunately, Emily's progress often didn't seem to match Joel's.

"You're so conceited!" Emily jabbed. "The only opinion you care about is your own."

Joel set his empty coffee mug down and leaned forward in his chair. The hair on the back of his neck prickled, and he placed his palms on the smooth wood of his kitchen table. He *hated* these fights.

"That's not fair, Emily," Joel countered. "I'm trying to hear you out."

"But you *never* agree with me!" Emily snapped. "You can say that you listen until you're blue in the face, but what does it matter if you never understand what I'm saying?"

A few months earlier, at about this point in the argument, Joel would've given in to her for the sake of ending the conflict. But things were different now. He steeled himself, exhaled a deep breath, and spoke calmly yet firmly to her.

"I can't accept that premise," Joel said. "I'm willing to have an honest conversation with you right now, but in order to do that, I need to ask that you take a breath and speak with me calmly."

Emily glared at him. "Who do you think you are? All you care about is winning the argument. You don't care about me or my feelings! You're just selfish!"

Joel had reached his threshold. He had to disengage. He stood up from his chair. "Emily, I feel like the conversation is elevating to a place in which I'm uncomfortable. When you're ready to talk in a respectful tone, let me know, and we can continue. Until then, I need to go to another room."

Joel moved toward the kitchen door, but Emily cut him off and stood in front of him, blocking his way.

"You're a coward," she uttered, her voice low and threatening.

The barb dug deep into his heart and caused him physical pain in his stomach. Even so, he replied calmly, "I'm sorry, but that's very hurtful to me. I'm going to my den. Will you please let me pass?"

He felt strange asking his much shorter, much smaller wife to let him leave the room, but he had no other good options. He refused to physically move her, but he also had no intention of staying in the kitchen with her. So asking politely was his only viable option.

Their gazes locked, and Joel remembered the love he'd seen in her eyes so many times before—while dating many years earlier, the night when he'd proposed to her, on their wedding day. Then he'd seen it later for the births of their children and numerous birthdays, anniversaries, and nights out celebrating victories over everyday life.

But now Emily's eyes burned with fury, a look more and more familiar over the last several years.

"Please, Emily?" Joel repeated.

With one last glare, she stepped aside.

As Joel walked past her and toward the stairs, Emily shouted from behind him, "Why won't you fight for our marriage?"

Joel didn't respond. He didn't slow his pace, nor did he fire back.

At Joel's lack of response, Emily cursed and stormed to the door. She grabbed her keys and went to her car, slamming the door so hard that it literally shook the house.

An hour later, Joel heard the garage door open and close, and then Emily's car door shut again. A fresh wave of anxiety hit Joel as he sat in his den.

She had come back, which was both good and bad. It was good because he knew she was home and safe. But virtually everything else about this situation remained an unknown for Joel.

Soon after, a knock sounded on the door.

"Come in."

The door opened, and Emily entered the room.

Joel turned away from the television and faced her. "How are you?"

She stood there, staring at him with her arms folded for a long, tense moment. Finally, she said, "You know, I was contemplating driving my car into a wall and just ending it."

Stunned, Joel said nothing, and Emily left the room.

<hr />

"I should've said something." Joel shook his head. "I froze. It was so shocking to hear that come out of her mouth."

Joel had gathered with a handful of his Life-Team members across town at the church of Pastor Vince. After Emily's suggestion that she was contemplating suicide, Joel didn't know what to do. He needed help, and he needed it fast. He had to know if he'd made a grave mistake.

"The pain in my life just keeps getting worse, and with Emily mentioning taking her life..."

His Life-Team members listened, waiting for Joel to finish.

"...but given how she's treated me in the past, I have to wonder if it's just more manipulation."

The Life-Team remained silent for another moment, and then Pastor Vince spoke up. "I would encourage you to err on the side of caution regarding what Emily has said. Threats or suggestions of this nature are a serious matter, so it makes sense to keep a close eye on Emily regarding any similar comments going forward.

"But I also want to affirm that this sort of threat could be another attempt to reestablish control in the relationship," Pastor Vince continued. "In these situations, the person who was the controller in the relationship—when faced with having to change—often stops at nothing to try to manipulate the other to resume their passive ways."

Joel's Life-Team affirmed Pastor Vince's words.

"I want to jump in, here, Joel," Max said, "to encourage you that you're on the right path despite how negatively Emily is reacting. You're doing great. Stay the course. This is what God is calling you to do, and this gives you the best chance of restoring your true self and your marriage. Will you allow us to pray for you right now?"

"Of course," Joel replied.

His Life-Team prayed for him, each of them taking a turn to ask for wisdom and guidance for Joel in specific areas of his life and relationship with Emily, and Joel received it all with an open heart.

Joel typically entered these conversations with great doubt, but today, as he had so many times before, he emerged from their meeting full of courage to press on.

IF YOUR WIFE EVER THREATENS SUICIDE, IMMEDIATELY SEEK PROFESSIONAL ADVICE AND HELP.

Your Doubts

If you've read this far, you might be in a difficult spot that will require you to make some changes... changes in your thinking, demeanor, outlook, and behavior. These changes typically prove difficult to make because they go against things you believe are true.

As a result, you will naturally face doubts along the way. A Life-Team can speak truth to you during these times.

Encouragement

During one particularly rough period in which Joel seriously doubted the changes he had been exhibiting due to the negative ways in which Emily was reacting, Joel emailed Chris—one of his mentors —with an update. Chris responded with this:

> Joel,
>
> I can't imagine the feelings you must have and how lonely and alone you must feel. I want to encourage you to continue to listen to what God is telling you and to work on yourself.
>
> My observation is that you've been doing an incredible job of that, especially in the midst of what you've been dealing with. I see you doing exactly what you need to be doing at this juncture. It probably doesn't seem like it, but this is the best chance for you to get healthy and your marriage to thrive. I don't have any idea how this will all work out, but we can be 100% certain that God is trustworthy.
>
> Continue to trust that God is for you and has your, and Emily's, best interests at heart. I know it's sometimes difficult to understand, but this is true even in the midst of circumstances that seem impossible to you. During these times God will continue to work in ways that you could never begin to imagine.

Joel put his head in his hands and wept and thanked God for Chris and the other amazing people He had placed in Joel's life. How could he walk this path without them? It encouraged him to have people who understood what he was dealing with.

In Joel's story, his Life-Team—which I was privileged to be a part of—encouraged him in multiple ways to move forward in doing some extremely uncomfortable things that, truthfully, didn't seem biblical (because of Joel's faulty beliefs).

However, he could move forward with much greater confidence

and courage because he regularly received confirmation that this was the correct path.

EN-**COURAGE**-MENT

Encouragement is an interesting word. Have you ever noticed that the word *courage* is embedded in *encouragement*?

Like Joel, I have a team of people who pour into me and help me—and challenge me—about who I am in my relationships—they're my Life-Team. At times, I've felt as if they literally poured courage into me.

Do not discount the value of walking with other safe people through this battle.

I HAVEN'T SEEN ANYONE SUCCESSFULLY NAVIGATE THIS TERRAIN BY THEMSELVES.

If you want to be the best husband you can be, if you want to be the best man you can be, then you must have a Life-Team. So man up and find one. You weren't made to do life alone!

If this is difficult for you or you can't seem to find the right people, go to Chapter 16, **You're Not Alone**, for some helpful ideas.

10

HEALING & LOVING CONFRONTATION

J oel continued on the path outlined in Chapter 9 for six months. His doubts persisted as Emily acted out more severely, and he sometimes reverted to his old way of thinking. But because of his Life-Team's support, he stayed on track most of the time.

Though he endured tremendous pain, he felt closer to God than at any other time in his life. He prayed for Emily—and himself—more than ever before. He heard from God through the Bible, through his Life-Team, through circumstances, and through a small voice in his spirit. These "words" would often be confirmed in multiple ways.

He came to view God as a great friend who would never leave him or forsake him.

HE WAS BEGINNING TO FEEL MUCH MORE SECURE IN HIS RELATIONSHIP WITH HIS HEAVENLY FATHER.

One day, Joel felt compelled to study the life of David in the Bible. He thought that maybe it was because he had just heard a teaching about him and he wanted to learn more.

As he dove into David's story in 1 and 2 Samuel, he noticed a pattern: people repeatedly treated David poorly. His brothers, his father, King Saul (who continually tried to kill him), his wife Michal, and others.

This observation fascinated Joel as he read those passages again and again, and he spent lots of time asking God about them. And God spoke and ministered to Joel in those times.

Joel carved out time each day to reflect on the passages about David and to journal his observations and anything God was saying to him. He earnestly sought God for any and every possible answer.

Joel then made a decision to seek God with a renewed fervor about his marriage and why he was so afraid of conflict. He asked his Life-Team to keep him accountable so he didn't back out at the last minute.

Thank God for Max.

Joel had caught himself thinking those four words repeatedly in the six months since his emergency meeting at Max's office. They'd met several times since then as well, and after each meeting, Joel left feeling inspired to stand up for himself and fight for his marriage in a whole new way.

Had it not been for Max's suggestion that Joel disengage, nothing would've changed in Joel's marriage—or within Joel himself, for that matter. The simple act of disengaging from Emily had given Joel his life back.

Prior to meeting with Max, Joel had given up virtually everything he held dear in order to spend more time with Emily. He'd done so willingly in hopes that spending more time with her could help resolve some of their issues. Instead, things had gotten worse.

Now Joel had resumed some of his pastimes and hobbies. He'd taken his son fishing four times since that first meeting with Max. He'd joined a community softball team for the fall season and played on Monday nights. He'd even managed to log a couple of hours in an old side business he'd started years ago, making wooden furniture.

It rejuvenated him. He hadn't felt so emboldened and free in years.

Thank God for Max.

But it wasn't all sunshine and rose petals. The act of disengaging had taken its toll on Emily, and it seemed like she'd been lashing out at him more frequently—and more severely. Because of her behavior, Joel sometimes slipped into his old patterns of behavior in order to placate her or avoid confrontation.

It bothered him, because the times in which he successfully disengaged, he felt closer to God, and he felt better equipped to deal with his marriage. So why did he keep reverting back to his old, ineffective methods of coping?

One day as he drove to his next meeting with Max, Joel pleaded with God to reveal where his fear of conflict originated. During the appointment, he said to Max, "I really want to get to the root of this issue with conflict. I know it's holding me back in my marriage."

"Okay." Max nodded. "Then let's do it."

Max prayed for them and then asked Joel to relax and sit quietly with his eyes closed. Then he encouraged Joel to ask God to reveal the origin of his fear.

Joel felt strange praying for this specific thing in front of Max, but he did as Max instructed. He squirmed in his chair and wondered what would happen if he didn't hear, feel, or see anything. He paused and asked Max about it.

Max replied, "That's okay. Not everyone hears, feels, or sees something. It's no problem if that's what you experience."

So Joel closed his eyes again and prayed, *Lord, please reveal to me where this all began.*

Then a memory resurfaced in Joel's mind—a memory from junior high school.

"You little skag." Don shoved Kyle against a locker, and Barry, Don's friend, held him there. "Look at you. So dopey. Why are you breathing my air?"

"Yeah, why are you breathing my air?" Barry repeated.

Joel swooped in from the side and separated Don and Barry from Kyle. He'd seen the whole thing from down the hall and knew he had to do something.

"Back off," Joel said as firmly as he could muster, positioning himself between them. Joel wasn't the biggest kid, but Kyle was his friend; he couldn't just let these jerks pick on him.

Don shoved Joel back into the locker. "Don't touch me, freak."

"Yeah, don't touch him," Barry echoed. "Who do you think you are?"

"Just the skag's idiot friend." Don scoffed.

Joel wanted to push Don back, but he didn't. He just held his ground. "Just leave him alone."

"Whatever," Don said. "You'll get what's coming to you, Jo-*elle*."

"Yeah. You'll get yours," Barry said.

As they walked away, they high-fived each other.

"*They're* the idiots," Kyle said just loud enough for Joel to hear.

Joel nodded. "Without a doubt."

"Thanks," Kyle said.

"No problem," Joel said. "We should probably get to class."

"Lead the way."

———

The next morning before school started, Joel opened his locker and slid his backpack inside. As he started to close it, footsteps squeaked on the linoleum floor behind him.

When he turned back, something wet splattered on his face and hair. He covered his face with his hands, surprised and confused. Then the heavy, overly-sweet scent of flowers hit his nose.

He caught a glimpse of Don and Barry through his squinted eyes, each of them shaking small glass bottles—one pink, and one clear—at Joel.

Perfume. Ladies' perfume.

Joel ducked away and scampered down the hall, but they'd already doused him with it. Worse still, he'd left his locker open, and instead of chasing Joel, Don and Barry had poured the rest of the perfume onto his backpack.

"No! Stop!" Joel shouted, looking around for a teacher, the principal, a custodian—anyone who could stop them.

No one came.

With their bottles emptied, Don and Barry turned toward Joel. "How do you like that, Jo-*elle*?" Don taunted.

"You smell like a sissy girl!" Barry crooned.

"Sissy girl! Sissy girl!" they repeated in unison until Joel pushed past them, grabbed his books for his first class, slammed his locker shut, and ran for the bathroom.

Their taunts followed him long after he couldn't hear them anymore, and other students added to it.

To make matters worse, later that day, in gym class, Barry grabbed Joel from behind, locked his arms down, and held him in place. Don was ready for it, and he grabbed Joel's right nipple with his fingers and twisted hard.

Joel yelped, and Don let go, but the damage had been done.

Barry let him go, and as he and Don laughed, Joel rubbed his bruised chest, fighting back tears.

Their "sissy girl" taunts resumed until the gym teacher finally got them to quiet down.

That night during dinner, a humiliated Joel explained to his parents what had happened. While his mother showed him sympathy, his father just scowled at him.

"So what did you do about it?" his father asked.

Joel shrugged. "Nothing."

"You didn't fight back?"

Joel shook his head.

His father leaned forward. "You just let it happen?"

Joel just stared at his mashed potatoes.

"So why should I feel sorry for you?"

"Alan…" Joel's mother started.

"No, Sally," Joel's father said. "I won't hear it. My house smells like the cosmetics department at Macy's because Joel wouldn't stand up for himself."

Joel gulped down his emotions. He wanted to cry.

"You need to learn to fight like a man," his father continued. "Otherwise those boys were right when they called you a 'sissy girl.'"

Those words had crushed Joel back then, and they still weighed on him now, so many years later. He looked up at Max, whose eyes showed great compassion. Joel explained what he'd just remembered, and they began to discuss it.

"Sounds like we've found the origin of your fear of conflict," Max said. "That day with Don and Barry was the start, and your dad's confirmation of those boys calling you a 'sissy girl' cemented that mentality in you. I want you to do something for me. I want you to write down the feelings that you felt or are still feeling about this story."

As they talked further, Joel began to piece together the chain of events and what God was showing him. He wrote down the following:

1. I challenged the bullies
2. The bullies made my life miserable and painful
3. Therefore, challenging anyone produces pain, so I must not challenge anyone

Max smiled. "Excellent! How about what happened with your dad?"

Joel thought about it in silence. Then he wrote down and shared his assessment:

1. My dad was disappointed with me
2. He said some tough stuff to me
3. I felt rejected
4. Therefore, disappointing others will lead to being rejected

IN THAT MOMENT, JOEL REALIZED
HIS GREAT FEAR OF BEING REJECTED.

Rejection was actually the root of Joel's fear of conflict—and his fear of disappointing others. His conflict with Don and Barry led to him feeling rejected—by them and others in the school. And disappointing his father also led to him feeling rejected.

"Great," Max said. "Now let's let Truth enter in. I want you to go back to those times in junior high with the bullies and with your dad and ask Jesus what He sees."

Joel did as Max instructed. Regarding the bullying episodes, he heard in his spirit,

"Joel, you are not a 'sissy girl.' What they say is not true. They're saying these things to you because I have made you to be a king, like David.

"Remember how people continuously attacked David? This is mostly because they feared him and were jealous of him. The same is true of you. I made you to be a mighty warrior like David."

Joel couldn't believe what he'd heard.

Was that really Jesus speaking to me or was it just in my mind?

Next, Joel saw Jesus standing behind his dad. Tears pooled in

Jesus' eyes, and He wore an expression that conveyed both pain and compassion.

Jesus spoke again, "My beloved son, you are worth everything to me. I would have died for you alone. Your father spoke from his own woundedness and didn't know what he was doing. He was wrong. You are a mighty warrior, and I love you immensely. Remember this, Mighty Warrior!"

Again, Joel was stunned. *Is this really Jesus or just heartburn from that pizza last night?*

Joel asked Max if it really was Jesus.

Max nodded. "This happens all the time with my clients. That was Jesus, and He wants to set you free."

Over the next three weeks, Joel shared this story with several members of his Life-Team. Each person nodded that his account truly sounded like the words of the Lord. They all believed that he had indeed heard from Jesus.

As a result, Joel gradually felt more and more emboldened about setting and maintaining boundaries with Emily. His doubts about disengaging dissipated, and he realized that Jesus was healing him of his fear of conflict and his fear of rejection.

Now, when Emily would shout things after him as he left the room, Joel just smiled, knowing that he was doing what was necessary.

My Story

I experienced something very similar to Joel.

A number of years ago, I decided to begin the year on a fast where I would not eat certain foods. I did this with the intent of focusing more on the Lord because I was desperate to hear from Him about my situation. I knew that He needed to do something in me to change my passive and timid ways.

One morning, I had decided to carve out an hour to sit with God, read His word, pray, and listen. Before I knew it, I was remembering back to a time when I was a sophomore in high school. I was sitting on my parents' couch in our basement with my first girlfriend, Kelly. It felt like I was literally there, reliving this moment.

I could even see what I was thinking: *She's so beautiful and so amazing... why is she with me?* (It's amazing how insecure I was, and still am at times.)

Kelly and I were kissing, and I reached for her breast with my hand. She stopped me and said, "Whoa, you're moving a little fast aren't you?" (We had only been "going out" a brief time.)

I was embarrassed and stopped.

The next day, Kelly called to tell me that she was breaking up with me. Though this was only a memory, the intense pain in my heart sparked anew, and I realized how utterly devastated I was.

In that moment, I recognized this was a significant event in my life and that this is where the fear of rejection took root in me.

In addition, though I didn't know God at the time, I saw how He had used that moment for good in my life (even though I was wrong for attempting what I did). Because of my intense fear of rejection, I refrained from leading a promiscuous lifestyle. In order to keep from experiencing that pain again, I resisted my subsequent urges to "make a move" on another woman.

This explained so much to me about why I had avoided conflict, especially in my marriage.

At that moment, God liberated me from my fear of rejection. I can't explain it, but I literally became different—it was amazing! When I shared this healing work of God with those on my Life-Team, they agreed with my assessment.

Soon thereafter, I started to set boundaries and be more lovingly assertive, regardless of what the outcomes might be—even if it meant I might be rejected. I felt free for the first time in a long time.

Critical Point

If you have not heard from God before, as described in Joel's and my experiences above, I recommend that you find a counselor who is adept at facilitating such encounters. And whether it is with a counselor or on your own (like in my experience), it's very important that you share this with members of your Life-Team to get confirmation that this is from the Lord.

We live in a spiritual world with an adversary[1] called "the father of lies." He wants nothing more than to whisper things in your ear to take you off course. Without confirmation from your team, you could be opening yourself up to deception.

If you feel God leading you to do this with Him, please only do so if you have a Life-Team. I implore you not ignore this point.

Spelling It Out

A month after Joel's revelation in Max's office, he decided it was time to approach Emily. He found her sitting in the living room reading a magazine.

"Can I talk to you for a minute?" Joel asked.

Emily's jaw tightened, and she exhaled a sigh. "Sure."

Joel bit back his frustration and said, "Emily, I owe you a big apology. I haven't led you or our family in a God-honoring way. I've been extremely passive with you. It has hurt me, and it has hurt you and our relationship. I realized that this originated with something that happened in junior high."

Joel related the encounter with God that he'd had in Max's office, then he got on his knees before his wife and asked, "Will you forgive me?"

Emily's countenance shifted from apathy to compassion—something Joel hadn't seen from her in a while. She replied, "Of course I will. Thank you for sharing this with me."

"Thank you." With courage, Joel continued, "But here's the thing:

We've been in counseling for the past five years. During that time, we've identified areas for both of us to work on, but sometimes I feel you still have areas where you can grow.

"I feel I've been more than patient, and I've continued to pursue you, hoping that you'd stop doing some of the things that hurt me. So I'm asking you to begin working on those things. I'm not asking for perfection, but until I start seeing you moving in that direction, I can no longer pursue you."

"No longer pursue me?" Emily's eyes narrowed at him. "What does that mean?"

Joel folded his hands in his lap. "It means I won't be spending as much time with you, and I won't be talking with you as much."

"How is that supposed to help anything?" She glared at him.

"Our interactions have been toxic over the last several months. The last several years, in fact. Everything I've tried has failed, so I'm going to try this approach for a while."

Emily rolled her eyes. "Fine. If that's the way you want it." She started reading her magazine again and made air quotes with her free hand. "So what 'things' are you talking about?"

"For starters, I want you to stop the name-calling. I feel very hurt and disrespected when you do that. And I'd like you to stop telling others that I need healing. I'd like you to stop trying to be the Holy Spirit in my life by telling me what you think He's telling you I need to do—He can do that job on His own.

"I'd also like you to be more respectful toward me and act like you're on my team. There are a few more things—things we've discussed in counseling for years—but I hope this is a start."

"Okay. Thank you." Emily set her magazine down and turned on the television.

Joel had done it. He'd conveyed his feelings to Emily, and she'd actually listened to him. He had just crossed an important line because he was resolute about not pursuing Emily if she failed to make an effort to improve her behavior.

He'd said what he needed to say, so he went downstairs to his den, his heart pounding out of his chest.

———————

Not pursuing Emily meant two primary things to Joel: First, with the help of his Life-Team, he'd decided to live in the same house as Emily but to behave as if they were separated. He had to work up to that concept because it was so different from his normal way.

Second, he had to let go of any hope that they would have sex during this time.[2] This was extremely important because he knew— without facing this reality—that he could easily be tempted to fall back into his passive ways if Emily tried to use sex to get her way.

BUT JOEL WAS DONE TRADING
HIS SELF-RESPECT FOR SEX.

Joel stayed true to his word. For the next three weeks, he didn't pursue Emily because, unfortunately, her behavior didn't improve. In fact, it actually got worse.

However, Joel found greater personal freedom. He did what he could to keep his side of the street clean. He no longer tried to control the harmony in his marriage, and it felt wonderful... and a bit scary.

———————

After a few weeks of Joel's new approach, Emily sat down with Joel. "Why haven't you been hanging around me as much lately?"

Stunned, Joel responded, "Do you remember our conversation a few weeks ago?"

"What conversation?"

Joel restrained his frustration. Perhaps she had genuinely forgotten. Still, it demonstrated what he'd been trying to convey to her all along: that she had failed to show him an appropriate amount of respect.

He said, "The one where I apologized for the un-godly way I've been leading you and our family. You know, my passivity?"

"Oh, yeah. I forgave you for that." Emily continued, "So what does that have to do with you not being around me?"

"Well, do you remember what I said after I asked for forgiveness?"

"No." Emily looked at her fingernails.

Again, Joel was flabbergasted. *How could she forget that?* "The part about how I needed to see you making some effort to stop treating me hurtfully."

Emily snapped, "I wish you'd fight for our marriage!"

As Emily stood and stormed away, Joel sat there in disbelief. *Is this really what I'm supposed to be doing?*

Over the next week, Joel met with several members of his team, and they each assured him that he was doing great. He was on the right path. They also confirmed something Joel had been thinking: writing a letter to Emily with what he was asking for would be a good idea. This way he could refer Emily to it when necessary.

Joel realized that such an action meant drawing a line in the sand. But, he realized, his previous attempts to make his stance clear to Emily had failed to impact her in any lasting, meaningful way. So he pushed through his fear and began to craft a letter sharing his heart and exactly what he wanted and needed from Emily.

He ran the letter by Max and three other members of his Life-Team. They each gave him feedback, helped him refine his wording, and encouraged him that this was a courageous and necessary act.

With great trepidation, Joel left the letter on the counter for Emily before leaving the house for work. Throughout the whole morning, he felt a pit in his stomach whenever he thought about it. He wondered, *Did I do the right thing?*

Here are some excerpts from his letter[3]:

Dear Emily,

Over the past couple of months, I've been doing lots of praying, journaling, and thinking about us. God has revealed deep things about me and lies I have believed, which have led to unhealth in me and how I have related to you.

We discussed the fact that my fear of rejection has kept me in a place in which I haven't loved and respected myself enough, and that has led me to continually allow myself to be mistreated. I've realized that I made our marriage an idol. I placed our marriage above my devotion to God. In other words, I took it as my responsibility to keep the "peace" at all costs in order to save the marriage.

I recognize that this is pride with a capital P. I was trying to manage the outcome rather than do what was right. I also see the selfishness in this as my primary goal was to prevent pain. In addition, I've seen that I have not truly believed God is faithful to handle things (the things I was afraid of) if I would've been obedient to what He was calling me to do as a husband.

In the past, I felt that if I could just show you more of what I thought was love then things would turn around. As a result, I gradually gave up more and more things I used to do for me.

I've realized that this isn't really love, especially to me. In fact it has prevented me from truly loving you appropriately since we're called to love others as ourselves (since I wasn't loving me well, how could I love you well?). I was trying to show love by keeping a false peace.

I had an ungodly belief that gentleness, kindness and passivity would bring peace. I have come to understand that that's a huge lie. Yet since recently abandoning that lie and that lifestyle, I've discovered a level of peace that I didn't think was possible, and I believe this is just the beginning. (This is what I meant when I told you that I don't think I've ever been in a better place.)

These revelations grieve me deeply. I have repented before the Lord, and He has forgiven me. I would like to again ask for your forgiveness for this as I'm very sorry for how this has impacted our relationship.

However, I'm running from the above negative behaviors (including passivity) and false beliefs. I will no longer allow my identity to be sabotaged. I'm going to respect and love myself and not allow certain things that I've allowed in the past because of my fear of rejection.

All of this has led me to not pursue you (as we discussed last month). I feel that my pursuit of you hasn't been returned in like fashion. In the past, I continually tried to do more and more, especially after coming to Christ.

I now understand how much this has hindered the health of our marriage. I'm hoping to see this change, as outlined below. Until I begin to see some change (or until God instructs me otherwise), I'm not going to pursue you. I must do this for me, my health, and for the health of our marriage.

Before going forward, I want to tell you two important points. One, I'm in no way stating that I want out of our marriage. And two, I'm also not saying that I don't care about the health of our marriage.

In fact, the reason for this letter and the way I've been behaving is to hopefully help bring our marriage to a healthier place that honors God.

This is what I'm asking of you as my wife... that you:

- respect and support me and what I do
- aren't contentious and don't mock me, call me names, or swear at me
- are clearly on my team, support and appreciate me
- are willing to work at resolving disagreements
- receive input with gladness even if you disagree with it

- seek to understand my needs and my desires and seek to meet them as I have sought to meet yours
- view sex the way God does and not use it as a weapon or view it as something that you "give" to me as if it's something you possess
- allow the Holy Spirit to be the Holy Spirit—in other words, stop telling me what you think God is telling you I need to do
- allow me to be me... including allowing me time away from you
- respect my need to keep certain work-related things private
- respect my leadership role in our home rather than resisting it
- celebrate my success like you're a part of it (which you are)... in other words, not be envious
- are open to doing fun things with me that fill my tank as I am to doing the same with you
- are my help mate, are kind to me, and are rowing in the same direction rather than against me

Emily, though you may not feel that I do right now, I love you deeply. I believe with all my heart that I'm currently showing you love, though it's different than what we're used to. And, in doing so in this manner, I *am* fighting for our marriage—perhaps for the first time in a healthy way.

I desperately want our marriage to succeed and to thrive. However, I will no longer manage or try to control that outcome. I have placed our marriage on the altar and asked God to do whatever He needs to do.

Again, I love you very much.

Joel

When Joel returned from work, he found Emily watching television. She said in a very appreciative tone, "Thank you for my letter."

Confused, Joel went upstairs to change. *Did she read the same letter I left on the counter this morning?*

The Fallout

Emily screamed up the stairs, "You want perfection! No woman could do these things! I can't believe you… you're so unrealistic and selfish!"

Clearly, she was no longer thankful for Joel's letter.

Over the next several days, things had begun to unravel, and now they'd reached a climax.

But Joel stuck to his strategy and calmly disengaged—something he was becoming very adept at. Even so, as he closed the door to his den, he wondered, *Am I selfish? Am I looking for perfection? Is Emily right?*

Again, Joel went to his Life-Team. They told him that he was still on the right path and that he was doing the right and courageous thing.

"But how do you *know* I'm doing the right thing?" Joel asked Max during one of their sessions. "Sometimes it seems like my marriage is still just getting worse."

"I understand your concern," Max said, "but keep in mind that the mission here is not necessarily to fix your marriage. The mission is to fix yourself and get you to a better place. Then, as a result, hopefully your marriage will recover as well."

Joel nodded. He'd found a lot of joy in working on himself and reclaiming his freedom in life, but it wasn't always easy to keep that in mind while living with Emily.

"Your focus is on you, rightly, for the time being," Max continued. "Your marriage consists of two broken people trying to fix each other. The strategy we're employing is to fix you, and then we can begin to work through issues in your marriage from a position of strength and wholeness."

Max's words and the words of Joel's Life-Team encouraged Joel greatly. He felt so alone in his marriage and so confused, but his Life-Team gave him the confidence he needed and helped him feel loved.

In fact, he felt as if God was showing him love *through* his Life-

Team. He was so grateful... yet he kept enduring so much pain. *What would I do without these amazing people in my life?*

———————

The intensity in Joel and Emily's marriage increased over the next five months.

Emily would say things like, "When I pray for our marriage, I don't pray for me anymore because I'm healed. I only pray for your healing."

Joel felt he was being spiritually bullied and manipulated, but he resisted the temptation to cave. In his heart, he was seeking God more fervently than he ever had before. And, ultimately, if she were praying for him with any degree of earnestness, God would honor her prayers, too.

Her new mantra bothered Joel even more, though. She repeatedly said, "I don't need to change at all. You're called to love me no matter what!"

Hearing her say it again and again made Joel go numb. But at the same time, he experienced more freedom because of what God was doing in him and because his Life-Team continued to speak life into him.

During this time, Joel often sat in his den in the basement or on their patio in the back, reading the Bible and seeking God. One day, he was watching a leadership video from a pastor whom he respected.

This leader was talking about hiring and firing employees, and he mentioned how many Christians think it's wrong to fire people. (They often think it's not God-honoring.)

This pastor shared a verse:

Warn a divisive person once, and then warn him a second time. After that have nothing to do with him.
    ~Titus 3:10

Joel wondered, *Does this also apply to marriage?*

He then remembered that he had recently put a list together of places in the Bible in which we are told to separate from certain types of people (see Chapter 8). He found that in his journal and spent considerable time reviewing it.

Wow. I've really been trying to control the harmony in my marriage. Though he thought he had already done so, for the first time Joel truly released his marriage to God.

"Father, my marriage is Yours," he prayed. "Do whatever You need to do, and may Your will be done."

Then the thought struck him, *It's possible that our marriage may actually not make it.*

11

THE CHALLENGE & MOMENT OF TRUTH

Joel didn't realize it at the time, but deciding to truly turn his marriage over to God made a huge difference in his life.

Now, four months later, he continually experienced a level of freedom and joy that he didn't think was possible, given the painful state of things in his home. He was doing much better about not trying to manage the outcome of his marriage, and he felt 100 pounds lighter.

However, the same patterns continued: Emily routinely lashed out, and Joel peacefully removed himself from the scene.

"I'm really concerned about you and your mental health," Emily said. "I think you're sick and need some help."

Emily's words surprised Joel. She'd said them out of the blue while he was brewing his morning coffee in the kitchen, catching him totally off guard.

Had she actually meant what she'd said? Or was this just another tactic to get him to see things her way? He briefly considered if he might actually be mentally ill, then he dismissed the idea for its absurdity.

He discerned that this wasn't an earnest recommendation. It was a reach on Emily's part to regain a measure of control in their relationship—and a pretty underhanded one at that.

Joel calmly responded, "Thanks for letting me know. I'll give that consideration."

As Joel walked downstairs to his den with his coffee in-hand, Emily's screeching voice chased his steps. "Your peace is *not* helping this family!"

Joel smiled, but not out of spite. He'd prepared for these kinds of outbursts, and Emily had been displaying them more and more as of late.

According to his Life-Team, these reactions were to be expected; Emily had proven time and time again to Joel that she wouldn't play fairly in their marriage, so Joel had to change his approach. Her outbursts, combined with Joel's deep sense of wholeness and peace about the situation were markers indicating that he was on the right path.

"How are things going with Emily?" Ray, Joel's pastor, asked. They'd met for lunch that day to catch up at Joel's request.

Joel shared the latest, and Ray's countenance saddened.

"Carol and I have been praying diligently for you both." Ray asked, "Would it be helpful if the two of you came to our house to see if we can help?"

Joel replied, "It certainly won't hurt. I'll ask Emily if she'd be willing to do that."

"Great. I'm really proud of how you've been handling yourself recently, Joel. This can't be easy for you, but I want you to know that I'm here to help you however I can," Ray said. "Hang in there. God's got you and your marriage in his hands."

"Thanks, Pastor Ray," Joel said.

Later that evening, Joel approached Emily about the idea of meeting with Ray and Carol at their home. "I think it would be good for us to talk with them. They're good people, and they want the best for both of us."

Emily sighed. "Fine."

"Do you have concerns about it?" Joel asked.

"Remember how Carol was mentoring me a few years back?" Emily asked.

"Yes."

"We stopped because she wasn't spiritually mature enough to help me," Emily said. "So I don't know what good can possibly come from this meeting, but maybe they can talk some sense into you."

Joel bit his tongue. Ray and Carol were pastors who led an entire congregation of people into a deeper relationship with Christ every day. They were certainly capable of helping if Joel and Emily could both open themselves up to Ray and Carol's wisdom.

But did Emily's negative attitude about the meeting mean she had already erected some sort of wall in her heart? The fact that she was willing to go gave Joel hope, but her words tempered his confidence that they'd experience any significant breakthroughs.

Nonetheless, Emily had agreed, so they set a date.

The entire trip to Ray and Carol's house, neither Joel nor Emily spoke.

Joel had considered small talk or even delving deeper into how they might approach the meeting with Ray and Carol, but he remained silent. Emily had barely said a word to him even before they'd left the house. What few things she had said were laced with anger, so Joel had opted to disengage, even though he didn't want to.

Joel parked in Ray and Carol's driveway and escorted Emily to the front door. It had snowed that day, and though the walkway was shoveled and salted, it still looked precarious enough, so Joel offered his arm for Emily to take. She didn't accept it and walked ahead without him.

Dear Lord, what am I doing here? Joel thought to himself as doubt filled his chest. *Is this going to make any difference whatsoever? Or are we just going to end up wasting the evening?*

Ray and Carol greeted them at the door, invited Joel and Emily inside, and then directed them to a green sofa in the family room. When they all took their seats, Ray asked how he and Carol might be able to help.

Right after Pastor Ray finished his question, Emily said, "I'll start."

Joel eyed her. For being so quiet before and during the car ride over, she sure hadn't wasted any time getting the conversation started.

"Our marriage is in a bad place. It has been in a bad place for a while now, but lately it has gotten worse because of Joel's behavior," Emily began.

Joel sat back and listened carefully. He wasn't planning on arguing with her in front of Ray and Carol, but he also didn't want to tolerate her saying things that were blatantly untrue, either.

"I don't know what's gotten into him recently," Emily continued, "but he's been avoiding me. He hardly talks to me anymore, and when he does, the only things he says are hyper-critical and unloving."

Not exactly accurate. But Joel didn't interrupt her for it.

The only times he'd been critical were in his letter and whenever he asked her to make changes in her behavior. As for being unloving —well, he'd taken more time for himself, and he still deeply loved Emily, but he could understand why the distance he'd established between them would seem unloving even though he now saw it differently.

"It's gotten so bad that I'm starting to worry about his mental health," Emily said. "I've always suspected he had narcissistic tendencies, but lately he seems to have fallen into depression or something. Whenever I bring it up, he avoids talking about it."

Joel stayed quiet. Her accusations in front of their pastors hurt, but he didn't correct or confront her.

Disengage. Let her talk. You'll have your chance soon enough.

"Now I'm wondering if he might be seeing another woman."

Joel's head swiveled to face Emily. *Did she really just say that?*

Joel's commitment to his marriage had never wavered, but Emily had just insinuated that he was having an affair. Shocked, Joel wanted to fire back, but he clamped his mouth shut.

This last assertion was new. She'd never even once suggested it to him, so he surmised that she'd kept it close to her chest specifically to bring it up in this meeting. Perhaps she thought that if she could damage his character in front of Ray and Carol then they'd side with her.

It made sense from a strategic perspective, but only if her goal was to "win" the argument. The reality, Joel decided, was that it just demonstrated how little she truly respected him and how little she'd heard him over the last few years.

Even so, more than anything, her claim amused Joel. Sure, it bothered him that she was taking this approach, but it didn't demolish his self-esteem. That alone revealed to Joel how far he had come.

When Emily finished her laundry list of concerns, Ray asked, "You mentioned Joel is overly critical of you. Can you give me an example?"

Emily replied, "Joel wrote me this letter asking me to do things that aren't possible. I sent it to Carol earlier today, and I know you've read it, too. His expectations are way too high."

"Yes, I've read it," Ray said. "Do you agree, Joel?"

Joel shook his head. "No. I think my requests are pretty straightforward and achievable."

"Look," Emily said, "I feel like you're in a boat and you're asking me to row with you, but you won't even let me into the boat."

Joel considered her analogy. "I want you in the boat. I've been trying to invite you into the boat for years now, but I've felt you weren't interested in coming aboard."

Emily fumed at him. "How can I come aboard when you're giving me lists of requirements that I have to meet before I pick up an oar?"

Pastor Ray interjected, "To be frank, I'm proud of Joel for writing this letter. It took great courage for him to finally stand up and be assertive. In some ways, he's been a lousy husband—which sounds harsh—but because of his passivity, it's true. It appears he's making changes now, and I think that's wonderful."

Pastor Ray's "lousy husband" comment stung, but Joel couldn't deny the truth. More than anything, Joel was thankful he'd taken a different road and started learning a new way.

Emily shook her head and folded her arms. "I still think he's asking for far too much. It's unreasonable. Impossible. I'm not ever going to be that perfect."

Carol gently and lovingly chimed in, "Emily, no one is asking you to be perfect. What Joel is asking for is basic stuff. You can do it if you choose. We've worked with a lot of couples where one of them has messed up. When that person says, 'I'll do whatever it takes to make this work,' we know there's a good chance for restoration.

"That same sentiment and dedication is what your marriage needs from you right now. Joel has admitted his passivity and timidity and has started to make changes, but he still has work to do. The question now, Emily, is whether you're willing to make changes as well. The choice is yours."

———

About an hour later, they drove home, once again in complete silence until Emily finally spoke.

"Ray and Carol are wrong," she said. "They don't know me very well."

Frustrated, Joel said nothing. What could he say? Despite all he'd done, despite all the counseling and the multiple approaches and everything else, he felt as though he had still failed to break through to Emily.

At this point, what other options did he have left?

A Difficult Step

Feeling beyond hope, Joel reached out to some members of his Life-Team the next day. They each encouraged him to "draw one last line in the sand" and ask Emily if she was willing to work toward reconciliation or not.

The fear of their next argument sending their marriage into a death-spiral—and possibly divorce—nearly paralyzed Joel, but he knew he needed to do something else. He was doing the work to change himself, and now he had to ascertain if she had any desire to do her part or not.

Armed with courage from his team, he began to plan how to move forward.

Joel had written Emily that letter earlier in the year so he could always point her back to it, so she wouldn't forget. He'd referenced it several times with her. Though it hadn't affected as much change as he'd hoped, he decided to use the same approach and write a new letter to her.

Once completed, he approached Emily to share the new letter with her. Realizing it may be his last shot to save his marriage.

This time, though, he read it aloud to her in their family room:

Emily,

A few days ago you said that you wanted to row with me but that I needed to let you into the boat. I'm thankful you said this because I believe it's a great picture of our current situation.

You're right—I haven't allowed you in the boat lately. I desperately want to be in the same boat as you... I really do. However, I cannot let you in unless you truly are willing to row with me.

I love you greatly, and I know we make a good team when we row in the same direction. I really want that in our marriage. Unfortunately, we've been far from that for a long time.

With that said, I've identified two things that are necessary for the restoration process to begin in our marriage. These would demonstrate to me your willingness to start rowing with me.

First, I'm asking you to show respect to me. You can exhibit this through the way you talk with me, the way you talk about me to others, by not telling me how I need healing, by not swearing at me or calling me names, etc.

Second, I'm asking you to support me and show you're 100% for me. It seems common that when I bring something up that you don't agree with, you become adversarial and critical. It's as if resistance is an automatic response from you. This damages our relationship.

Currently, we're at a crossroads in our marriage. Regardless of where we go from here, our road ahead will be difficult. It will be painful at times and full of a lot of work for both of us.

But I want you to know that I love you very much, and I desire that we work toward rebuilding our marriage together.

Both of the above points are necessary for us to begin to build a new, undivided marriage relationship. So I come to you today to tell you that the choice is yours. I can't be in the same boat unless you choose to row with me.

Will you choose our marriage and decide to row with me or not?

I look forward to hearing what you decide.

Much love,
    Joel

When he finished, Emily scowled at him. "If I'm going to do these things, then I get things too."

Joel responded, "Then write down what you need, and show me."

"I will." Emily's expression softened, and she sighed and rubbed her forehead. "Joel, I really do love you, even if it doesn't seem like I do."

Joel bit back his emotions as tears stung the corners of his eyes. "I know you do. I love you, too."

"I want to try to get better. I want you to get better, too," she continued. "It's going to take a lot of work."

"It is. But we can get there together. Will you—" Joel swallowed the lump in his throat. "Will you row with me, Emily?"

12

FREEDOM BLUEPRINT

What Happened Next? (Joel & Emily)

While working with and encouraging Joel, I was very impressed with how he navigated these difficult waters and thought his story could be very instructive for anyone facing similar challenges.

In walking through this with him, I saw a humble, hurting man trying to do everything he could do to be the husband that God called him to be. He had serious issues, but he was willing to explore them and work on them with God. I haven't worked with many men who were as teachable and open to correction.

Many who hear this story immediately ask, "Well, what happened? Did they get divorced? Did Joel retreat back to his old way in an attempt to save the marriage? Did Emily decide to fight for their marriage and seek help?"

After about a week, Emily got back with Joel to tell him how sorry she was for the way she'd treated him. She committed that she *would* begin rowing with Joel—or at least try her best. She would seek to show him respect and support him. And Emily agreed go to counseling with Joel—and to see the counselor on her own.

Though suspicious, Joel was very hopeful. He hadn't seen this side of Emily in a long time. No matter what happened from here, they now shared some common ground.

As of this writing, it appears that their marriage has turned the corner. Joel has not retreated—at least most of the time, and Emily has mostly lived up to her commitments.

They are continuing to see Max on a regular basis, and Joel continues to seek God and meet regularly with his Life-Team. In addition, with Max's guidance, Emily has begun to build a healthy Life-Team of her own.

Joel knows that they have a long road ahead, and he now firmly believes his marriage will survive. However, he's no longer willing to try to control the harmony in his marriage by being passive and timid.

I was extremely hesitant to share this information. In fact, the early drafts of this book did not include it because I didn't want you to get caught up in the outcome. I often pray that Joel and Emily's marriage will continue to grow and begin to thrive.

However, I must remind you that even though Emily responded positively, it was not the metric by which Joel measured his success... and it isn't for you either. Joel achieved success because he stepped out of his comfort zone in faith in a way that honored God, and God met him there. He is doing great work in Joel, and as a result, Joel has regained much self-respect.

Sure, this is a happier ending than that of other couples. But had Emily not responded positively, Joel's life-change still would have been a success.

If you're an athlete, success is based on the scoreboard. If you're in business, it's based on the bottom line. And in our homes, we men inappropriately judge our success on how happy our wife is or how much harmony we experience in our relationship.

The truth is, we cannot control outcomes—that's God's job, and it's His alone. Our job is to obey Him and leave the outcomes to Him. This has become my definition of success. It has nothing to do with outcomes.

Some of the couples who go through a similar process end up reconciling and begin to build amazing, God-honoring marriages as Joel and Emily are doing. Others don't end so happily; sadly, some get divorced, and some men revert back to their old passive ways to keep the peace so as to avoid divorce.

> AS A WORD OF ENCOURAGEMENT AND HOPE, I NEED TO
> TELL YOU THAT I'VE NEVER MET A MAN WHO REJECTED HIS
> LIFE OF PASSIVITY—AS JOEL DID—AND REGRETTED IT.

However, one thing that's common with most men who choose to confront their passivity is that they faced tremendous adversity after doing so.

As a wise mentor once told me, "You have a choice. You can sign up for some difficult and immediate pain that might last for several years (but bring you to a healthier version of yourself), or you can choose a lifetime of dying day by day by a million paper cuts."

I've worked with many men in situations similar to Joel's. In my experience...

> THOSE WHO HAVE BEEN WILLING TO DO THE INTERNAL WORK HAVE
> EMERGED IN THE HEALTHIEST, MOST JOYFUL PLACE THEY'VE BEEN...
> REGARDLESS OF THE OUTCOME OF THEIR MARRIAGE RELATIONSHIP.

If you've read this far, you're probably at a crossroads. You have some big decisions before you. I pray for God's wisdom and His courage for you.

Blueprint of Joel's Steps to Personal Freedom

The following is a summary of some of the key actions Joel took along his journey to internal freedom:

- He began to seek God more earnestly, and he intentionally set aside time to do so.
- He began to journal regularly and write down things that happened between Emily and him as well as those things He heard God say to him. This helped him in many ways including getting appropriate feedback from his Life-Team, keeping his thoughts straight, and remembering what God had done for him as he looked back (like the Israelites did with the stones in Joshua 4:9–24).[1]
- He learned to set boundaries and disengage when his wife was harming him (see Chapter 8).
- He prayed regularly for his wife and for himself... for God to heal them both, to open their eyes, and for His will to be done.
- He assembled a Life-Team (including routine Christian counseling) to help encourage (to pour courage and truth into) him, and he remained open to their feedback. This also helped him to seek God more and to set healthy boundaries (see Chapter 9).
- With some of the members of his team, he explored the root causes of his faulty thinking—which led to his passivity—and sought God as to how to heal those areas in him (see Chapter 10).
- With the help of his Life-Team, he developed a plan to speak truth in love and share his needs with his wife (see Chapter 11).
- He truly put his marriage on the altar and gave it to God that He might do as He saw fit.
- He courageously continued to do the difficult things and

step into unknown and frightening territory with the help
and encouragement of his team.

- He made plenty of mistakes and went backward toward
passivity a number of times. But he recognized that he was
not perfect, and he moved forward again, also with the help
of his team.

In going through this process, Joel still wanted his wife to be
happy. However, he realized that making her happy wasn't the end-
goal and was outside of his control.

As husbands, we're not the source of our wives' happiness. Sure,
we're responsible for treating her well and protecting her, but we're
not responsible for her happiness. Her happiness is her choice (and
the same holds true for you and me).

Please know that this is not a "Seven-Step Plan to Wholeness."
This was one man's journey. Yours may look different, or you may
share similar experiences as Joel.

In addition to the summary above, Joel also discovered a couple of
other tactics which proved of great help to him...

The Sacred Pause

First, Joel learned how to *respond* rather than *react*. This became
both a critical step in Joel's journey and something that he said
brought him tremendous freedom.

In his time with the Lord, Joel found a verse in the book of James
that sparked this significant paradigm shift in his life:

*My dear brothers, take note of this: Everyone should be quick to listen, slow
to speak and slow to become angry.*
~James 1:19

As he pondered this verse, and as he discussed this with his team,
he had an "a ha" moment. He had always considered this to be

instruction to listen intently to whomever he was with and to listen more than he spoke.

However, as he looked at these instructions, he realized it didn't actually say to whom we are to listen. The verse also means that we're to be quick to listen to God.

One of his Life-Team members said, "I like to think of this as a 'sacred pause.' I pause to ask God how He'd like me to respond."

That idea resonated with Joel, and he decided to ask God to help him take his own sacred pause when the temperature increased in dialogue with his wife. Over time, he began to practice this, and it helped him to respond peacefully rather than reacting with anxiousness, anger, or by shutting down.

Fruit Inspectors

Second, Joel became a fruit inspector. Before that, he had lived his married life as a word inspector instead.

What, exactly, do I mean by these two terms? Perhaps the best way to show you is through an illustration.

Do you remember the *Peanuts* cartoons? Lucy would tell Charlie Brown that she would hold the football so that he could kick it. He'd run up as fast as he could, and just as he swung his leg, Lucy would snatch the ball away and he would land painfully on his back. This happened time after time, yet Charlie Brown kept attempting to kick it.

Charlie Brown was a word inspector. Though Lucy repeatedly didn't follow through on her commitment, Charlie took her at her word... even though she clearly wasn't trustworthy.

Had Charlie Brown been a fruit inspector, he would've looked at Lucy's behaviors to see if they lined up with her words.

PART OF BEING WISE IS ACCURATELY DISCERNING IF A PERSON IS TRUSTWORTHY. WE CAN'T ASCERTAIN THIS BY THEIR WORDS ALONE— WE MUST OBJECTIVELY EVALUATE THEIR BEHAVIORS.

Jesus told us that we, too, should be fruit inspectors:

"Watch out for false prophets. They come to you in sheep's clothing, but inwardly they are ferocious wolves. By their fruit you will recognize them. Do people pick grapes from thornbushes, or figs from thistles? Likewise every good tree bears good fruit, but a bad tree bears bad fruit. A good tree cannot bear bad fruit, and a bad tree cannot bear good fruit. Every tree that does not bear good fruit is cut down and thrown into the fire. Thus, by their fruit you will recognize them."
  ~Matthew 7:15–20

Did you catch that? He said that some people will come to you in sheep's clothing. In other words, they'll look like something they aren't, or they'll say things, but their actions won't align with their words. He said we should let their "fruit," or their actions, dictate what we are to believe about them.

In another passage, John the Baptist said this:

John said to the crowds coming out to be baptized by him, "You brood of vipers! Who warned you to flee from the coming wrath? Produce fruit in keeping with repentance. And do not begin to say to yourselves, 'We have Abraham as our father.' For I tell you that out of these stones God can raise up children for Abraham. The ax is already at the root of the trees, and every tree that does not produce good fruit will be cut down and thrown into the fire."
  ~Luke 3:7–9

John was warning those who were coming to be baptized that baptism alone or claiming Abraham as their father would not help them in eternity. They needed to produce fruit in keeping with repentance.

In other words, if they truly were repentant, their fruit—or the way they lived their lives—would be evidence of that change in their lives. He wasn't saying perfection is the standard. No, it was simply a heart of repentance... one that was quick to ask for forgiveness and turn away from sin. That is true repentance.

As time went on, Joel became much more adept at not falling for the allure of Emily's promises to "hold the football down this time." He began to inspect his wife's fruit rather than her words of promise. This brought much greater clarity and peace to his life.

Now that we've looked at the blueprint, we want to be careful of land mines that can trip you up. In this next section, I'm going to show you how to avoid these pitfalls.

The Pendulum

I've made a number of drastic changes in my life. Sometimes I did this poorly—especially when I was a young man. I had a tendency to over-correct.

For example, before becoming a Christ-follower, I thought that accumulating finances was the key to security and peace. Boy was I wrong. It seemed the more I accumulated, the less secure I felt and the more stress I experienced.

Then I came to understand that God was the only source of true security and peace. As a result, I began to ignore my finances and lose money. I had over-corrected.

In other words, the pendulum swung too far to one side—and to correct it I moved it all the way to the other side. Healthy living comes when the pendulum is moving toward the center—toward balance.

As you work through these changes in your attitude, your thinking, and your behavior, you might be tempted to over-correct.

The moment some men—who have been passive and timid for most of their lives—begin to break free from that, they're in danger of the pendulum swinging too far to the other side. One example of this would be moving from passivity toward arrogance and/or dictatorship. This is equally bad.

Beware of this human tendency and talk through these things with your Life-Team. Ask them to point out any over-corrections.

Proverbs 11:17 tells us, "A kind man benefits himself, but a cruel man brings trouble on himself."

Throughout this process, please do yourself a favor and be kind. Don't let the pendulum swing too far, causing you to be cruel. It will only bring you trouble.

Anger

Because of the abuse and/or mistreatment you've received, it's quite possible for you to be feeling anger. If you feel this way, you're not alone. It's quite common.

> *In your anger do not sin.*
> *~Ephesians 4:26*

The above verse indicates that being angry isn't the issue. However, what we do with that anger is critical.

When you feel anger, it's important for you to release it. Otherwise it will come out in ways you don't intend toward others, or it can affect your health.

The most appropriate person to vent to is your Father, God. If the thought of venting to God sounds like heresy, read the Psalms. King David vented to his Father in many of them. And God said of David that he was "a man after my own heart" (see Acts 13:22). God can take it. Bring your anger to Him.

Another group with whom you can process your anger is your Life-Team.

Whether it's with God, your Life-Team, or both, whatever you do, get your anger out. Otherwise it may come out elsewhere. Venting your anger toward your wife, your kids, or others will not help your situation.

A note of caution: many men who harbor a fear of rejection and behave in a passive way view being firm or disagreeing with their wives as being angry or mean. This simply isn't true.

You will need to be firm in order to stop accommodating your wife in her dysfunction. But you can do so without being angry or mean.

Another One in Sight?

During this season you'll be in a very vulnerable spot. You probably won't experience much intimacy in your home, either emotionally or physically. As a result, when another woman begins to show you respect and shows interest in you, it can feel amazing. You may even begin to feel like a man again.

Be very careful. This is one of our enemy's greatest ploys, and it's a counterfeit. Sure, you may experience some temporary pleasure, but it will only hurt your ability to become free, and it will greatly and unnecessarily complicate your situation.

If you struggle with temptation during this time, please confide in members of your Life-Team, even if it's only one person on your team. Check in with them regularly, ask them to check in with you regularly, and have them ask you the tough questions. I promise you, you'll be so glad you did this.

What if Things Don't Go Well?

If you decide to make the courageous decision to reject your passivity, I applaud you. You're entering into uncharted waters in your life. But be encouraged—the Lord is with you! He loves to meet us in rough waters. Think of Jesus meeting Peter on the stormy seas (see Matthew 14:22-33)!

If you decide to move forward in this, you've probably counted the cost (see Luke 14:28). You understand that you can no longer control outcomes, and you understand that your marriage is now in the hands of God.

I'll warn you that you may experience powerful emotions that you've rarely experienced since childhood. You may have even spent your whole life trying not to feel these emotions.

It will likely be difficult, yet at the same time it can be immensely rewarding. You'll probably want to revert back to your passive self to alleviate the pain. It's in these times that you especially need to lean into your Life-Team.

HAVE I EMPHASIZED THE IMPORTANCE OF NOT OVERLOOKING YOUR LIFE-TEAM?

Please don't skip this step. I haven't met any man who's successfully navigated these waters without a healthy support system in place.

Many think that asking for help is a sign of weakness. It's actually a sign of strength and humility.

So Assemble Your Team!

If you'd like some assistance with this, please refer to Chapter 16: You're Not Alone.

As you progress through the things you feel God is leading you toward, you may find yourself at the "end of the line." You may sense that separation or divorce is your only option.

IF YOU FEEL GOD IS LEADING YOU TOWARD DIVORCE, DON'T DO THIS ON AN ISLAND. DON'T BE A LONE RANGER. DON'T ISOLATE. BUILD A LIFE-TEAM AND REACH OUT TO THEM![2]

Don't make this decision lightly or quickly. Work through this with your Life-Team. Don't move toward divorce unless you have a strong word from the Lord and your team confirms this.

On your FREE Bonus Site (see the front or back of the book) there are many resources that have been helpful to couples in restoring their marriages. If you are in danger of divorce, I would highly encourage you to talk about these resources with your Life-team and ask them for recommendations.

Divorce is a huge, life-altering decision that affects a lot more people than you and your spouse. Do not rush into it.

[13]

BREAKING THE CYCLE

The instructions and encouragement in this book aren't just about you, your wife, and your marriage. They're also about your kids, their future selves, their future mates, and their future marriages. You're an example to them of what it means to be a husband and a father as well as what a marriage looks like.

You might be feeling like you've modeled the wrong thing to your kids and to others. If this is the case, fear not. No one has been a perfect spouse or parent. And God is the God of restoration. He can restore you no matter what your current situation looks like.

As you begin to seek Him and follow the steps outlined in this book, you'll make changes that will be very apparent to those observing you (your kids, your wife, and others).

Remember, your wife may not react positively to some of your changes—but that is *not* an indicator that you're on the wrong path. Even your kids might experience some fear because of how differently their dad is behaving. Again, this is to be expected.

You're embarking on a journey to not only change you but also to change your generational line from this point forward.

You now have the opportunity to model a godly husband which will impact your family for generations. Making this shift out of passivity will be a great testimony to your family. You have sought God, and He's making radical changes in you.

YOU'RE ON A COURAGEOUS JOURNEY THAT WILL IMPACT YOUR GENERATIONAL LINEAGE!

If you have grown children, and even if you now have grandchildren, all is not lost. You can begin to model it now. It's never too late. God is the God of second chances. He is the Great Redeemer. He can and will redeem your situation when you walk in His ways.

Passivity & Bullying | Fathers & Sons

Years ago during the first week of school, Robert, my seventh-grade son, came home looking more dejected than I had ever seen him. He went upstairs to his room and shut the door. I followed him, knocked on the door and asked to come in. He said I could.

I saw him lying on his bed quietly sobbing into his pillow. My heart sank.

I sat on his bed, put my head on his back, and asked what was happening.

Robert explained that some boys at school had sprayed him with bug spray and kept punching him in the shoulder all while making fun of him in front of the rest of the class. He continued through tears, "Dad, nobody likes me. They all think I'm stupid!"

HIS WORDS PIERCED MY HEART. I DIDN'T KNOW WHAT TO DO SO I JUST HELD HIM AND CRIED WITH HIM.

Over the next several months, my wife and I watched our son become a shell of the fun-loving kid we had known. It crushed us.

We met with the principal of the school who assured us that

things would be taken care of. However, the bullying continued, and our son continued to suffer.

One morning I awoke and remembered a dream I had—which is unusual for me. I usually don't remember my dreams.

In this dream, Robert and I were biking in the mountains. I was a bit ahead of him and came upon a scenic overlook. I stopped there to take in the view and waited for my son.

He came upon me a little too fast and didn't slow down in time. I watched in horror as he plunged over the edge into a deep canyon below.

I woke up in a sweat with my heart pounding out of my chest. I knew this dream was significant. As I thought and prayed about it, I concluded that God was trying to tell me that this was a pivotal time in the life of my son. That he was "headed over the cliff" unless something changed. I sensed God telling me that I needed to be the change agent.

I shared this with some trusted others who felt like this was exactly what God was saying. I felt that I had no choice. Though I wasn't sure what to do, I knew I needed to be much more intentional about sowing into the life of my son.

I began to research and ask others for ideas about what to do. During this time, I was in a men's group, and we'd been going through a three-year study about authentic manhood.[1] In the first year of the study, the author shared four keys to living as an authentic man. The first was this:

AN AUTHENTIC MAN
REJECTS PASSIVITY.

At the time, I was unaware of how passive I truly was. But I knew this was a good place to start with Robert.

He and I met weekly to talk, read, or watch a video together. These were typically based on rejecting passivity but also included sessions about sexual purity.

My son typically wasn't excited about these times together, but I could tell he kind of liked them. I occasionally got frustrated with him because he appeared so disinterested, and I assumed he wasn't paying attention at all. But months—and sometimes even years— later, he would make a comment about something we had discussed previously, and that encouraged me.

We ended up moving Robert to a different school to give him a fresh start. However, his wounds from the bullying were still evident to his mom and me.

Ceremonies and Blessing

From when he was 12, I continued to pour into my son whenever I could. We've taken annual trips to watch our favorite college football team play a road game. We've also taken hiking trips to the mountains and gone to concerts together. All for the purpose of building him up and having fun together.

I did several ceremonies for him along the way to indicate his path to manhood. In between his 17th and 18th birthday, Robert and I— along with seven other guys—hiked to the top of a mountain and spent the night.

While at the summit, each of the men spoke into Robert's life and we inducted him into manhood. I gave him an inscribed sword to commemorate the occasion. He was a bit stunned, and I'm not sure he knew what was happening.[2]

A couple of years later, he began to encounter some relational difficulties at work. He told me one day, "Dad, thank you so much for teaching me the importance of rejecting passivity! I see so many passive guys my age that I can't believe it. And I see how easy it is for me to fall in those ways. I really appreciate all you've done for me."

I'll never forget that day. It felt like God was blessing me abundantly.

To this day, my son—who's now married and on his own— continues to seek input from me on different situations. He also tells me from time to time, "Dad, thank you so much for all you've done for me. I know I didn't appreciate it at the time, but I sure do now!" What a blessing that is to me. As I write these words, I do so with tears of gratitude in my eyes.

I'm quite certain that if God hadn't given me that dream about Robert, and had I not followed through on His prompting, the above story could be very different.

I share this not to brag. Rather, I do so to encourage you. I was clueless. Yet by God's grace, we navigated this time together.

I want to make one thing very clear here: While being intentional with my son for those 10 years, I was oblivious to the depths of my own passivity and timidity. My point is that you don't need to be healed and perfect to pour into your kids—or to invest into anyone else for that matter.

You, too, can do this. And what a difference it will make in your family for generations!

Start Early, But Now Is The Best Time

Obviously, the earlier we can begin to instill these values in our sons, the better. However, many of us are older when we get this revelation about rejecting passivity. Some of us may even have sons who are no longer living at home.

Is it too late? No. No matter what or when, now is the time to begin.

The best way to impart this to your son(s) is by living it. So begin there and model it to them. Then ask God to reveal how you can sow this message into their lives.

I've given a couple of ideas above as to how to do this. And if you have older sons, perhaps a conversation like this might be a way to get the ball rolling:

"I need to ask for your forgiveness. I'm coming to understand that I've been very passive in our home, and I know that in a way, I modeled this to you. I'm so sorry for this. Will you forgive me?"[3]

Then you can ask him if there's a way you could share some of what you've been learning and go from there. Or maybe God will give you another way to do this. In any case, remember that it's not too late.

This is critical for our sons at any age. It can help to prepare them to be themselves in their relationships and not be tempted to fall into passivity and codependency... to be someone they aren't just to win the approval of others.

A MAN GETTING MARRIED WITH A FOUNDATION
OF PASSIVITY CAN LEAD TO A DESTRUCTIVE MARRIAGE.
WE CAN HELP OUR SONS TO AVOID THAT.

[14]
THE ONLY WAY

It's highly probable that you're reading this book out of your desperation to get answers for your marriage. And it's quite possible that you don't have a relationship with God. You may not even believe He exists. On the other hand, you may be someone who has spent much of your life in church.

In either case, or at any point in between, I'm so thankful that you're here and that we're talking now.

The principles I share in this book are based on biblical truth. The thing about many biblical principles is that they're equally true for people who don't believe in God just as they're true for those who follow Jesus. So if you're not a believer in God or the truth of Scripture, the concepts taught in these pages will still help you.

However, I would be remiss if I didn't explain that they will help you only to a point. For *true* transformation and healing to take place in your life, it must occur in relationship with Jesus.

I ask that you hear me out on this; I'm not sharing this for my benefit but rather because of my love for you. As someone who has spent much of his life deceived about certain things, I know how easy it is to miss this point.

Whether you're a follower of Jesus or not, I highly encourage you to read the following excerpt from my book, *Calming the Storm Within: How to Find Peace in This Chaotic World* in which I describe how the Christian faith can be summarized by two words: *Substitutionary Atonement.*

Substitutionary Atonement

Let's look at these two words. *Atonement* is "payment for an infraction" while *Substitutionary* means "to take the place of." In other words, the Christian faith is all about Someone Else paying for our infractions. Christianity is the only religion in the world in which this is true. *All others preach self-atonement.*

In God's eyes, blood must be shed any time sin occurs. In fact, the law requires that nearly everything be cleansed with blood. Without the shedding of blood, there is no forgiveness (see Hebrews 9:22). So let's look at some Old Testament stories to see how this played out.

In Genesis 3:21, when Adam and Eve first sinned, God came down and killed an animal to provide clothing. Blood was shed (in this case, from an innocent third party—an animal).

God once told the Israelites to kill their prize lambs and spread the blood from the lamb on their doorways so that He would know to "pass over" their house and not kill their firstborn sons and animals. Blood was shed because of sin, again, from an innocent third party (see Exodus 12).

In Leviticus 16, we learn of the Day of Atonement. On this day the community gathered around the high priest and two goats. The priest sacrificed one of the goats, again shedding blood from an innocent third party.

Next, the high priest ceremonially transferred the sins of all the people to the second goat. Then they released the goat into the wilderness to die, signifying that their sins had been atoned or paid for. (This is where we get the term "scapegoat," by the way.)

In the New Testament, in John 1:29, we see John the Baptist say,

"Look, the Lamb of God, who takes away the sin of the world!" In other words, John was saying, "Look, here comes our scapegoat!"

Fast-forward to the cross. Just as Jesus breathed His last, He said, "It is finished." (John 19:30) Jesus didn't say this because He was giving up. He was saying, "It's done. The atonement has been paid for all mankind."

So why do we need this atonement?

Romans 3:23 says that all of us have sinned and fallen short of the glory of God. Every single one of us. As a result, our sin separates us from God because He can't be in the presence of sin. He is a Holy God. Obviously, this isn't good news for us, as we've all sinned.

As if this wasn't bad enough, Romans 6:23 tells us that the wages of sin is death. So what we're due, our "paycheck," so to speak, is death. Not just a physical death but an everlasting, spiritual death completely separated from our Heavenly Father. Not pretty.

However, Romans 10:9 gives us hope: If you confess with your mouth, "Jesus is Lord," and believe in your heart that God has raised Him from the dead then you will be saved.

Here's the rub: what Romans 10:9 discusses is the exact opposite of a wage. It's a gift. We cannot earn it. We can only choose to receive it or reject it.

When we choose to receive this gift from God, the gift that Jesus paid for us, He not only allows us to live with God in Heaven for eternity but He also enables us to be fully alive, here and now (see John 10:10). He gives us a way to find peace with God, the peace that transcends all understanding.

I don't know about you, but I don't want anything to do with a wage of death (an eternal death). I want the gift that Jesus gave, which is eternal life and life to the full.

In Revelation 3:20, Jesus says, "Here I am! I stand at the door and knock. If anyone hears my voice and opens the door, I will come in and eat with him, and he with me." He stands at the door and knocks. He is a gentleman. He won't force His way in.

He's waiting for you. So you have a choice to make. You can

choose to open the door and accept the gift that Jesus has for you, or you can choose not to *which is actually rejecting Him.*

Because God gave us free will, we all have a choice. Either we will choose to accept Christ for who He is or we will choose to reject Him. There is no middle ground.

The tough part is this: choosing to accept Jesus as your Lord and Savior is not the easy path... at least not in this life on earth. This isn't just a ticket to Heaven which allows you to continue with life as usual.

In my opinion, we mess this up in the Church. We tell people they can say a certain prayer and be "saved." (In fact, I don't see anywhere in the Bible where a "prayer" is necessary for salvation.)

Instead we focus on the "and you will be saved" part of Romans 10:9 while forgetting the "Jesus is Lord" part of that same verse. If someone is your lord, you follow them and obey them. When we commit to this relationship with Jesus, we're in essence committing to an exchange: our life for the life of Jesus.

If you make this commitment it means you'll have some scary moments; Jesus said so. It may make you feel extremely unsafe and unsure at times. You may face pain and heartache. He may ask you to do things you don't want to do.

But the good news is that living your life through Him is guaranteed to be much richer, fuller, and more meaningful than a life lived without Him.

Though it may feel unsteady at times, resting in His arms is truly the safest place you can be, and it brings a peace you never thought was possible.

If you haven't made this commitment, I encourage you to do so now. Simply make your own commitment from your heart. Jesus knows your heart, so he'll know if you mean it. It could sound something like this:

"Jesus, I need help and forgiveness. I can't save myself. Only You can. Thank you for dying for me and for being my scapegoat. I want You to be my Lord. I

commit from this day forward to serve You, to follow You, and to obey You. Please show me the way to do all these things."

If you haven't made this decision, would you stop reading right now and ask yourself what is stopping you? I'm very serious about this. Put the book down for at least a day and really ponder this question:

WHAT IS KEEPING ME
FROM FOLLOWING JESUS?

Write down all the reasons. Ask God to show you the way. Find a mature Christian who can talk through this with you.

I cannot stress this enough. This commitment is critical not only for your eternal destination but also for the peace you experience on this earth. Until you make this decision, it will be impossible to find the peace that God desires for you.

So again, please put the book down and come back to this spot when you have made that decision or when at least a day has passed. I even put a line on the page to show you where you left off…

_____

If you've decided to welcome Jesus as your Lord and Savior, congratulations! Angels are rejoicing in Heaven (see Luke 15:10), and your name is now written in the Lamb's Book of Life (see Revelation 20:15).

You have a new identity. The Holy Spirit now resides inside of you and will give you the desire to glorify God. It's crucial that you tell some others about your commitment—the verse I mentioned earlier said, "If you confess with your mouth…"

Tell someone you know who is a believer. This will really encourage them, and they can help you to take the next steps.

Keep in mind that this isn't something to take lightly. You've made a commitment to the Creator of the Universe that Jesus is your new Lord, your CEO, your Boss. Anytime you get a new boss, you want to find out what he wants you to do, right? No different here. You'll want to find out how to walk with Him and follow Him.

It's important to realize that you weren't meant to go on this journey alone. You were meant to travel with others.

> *Two are better than one, because they have a good return for their work: If one falls down, his friend can help him up. But pity the man who falls and has no one to help him up! The fact is that others can help you when you stumble.*
>
> ~*Ecclesiastes 4:9–10*

They can also challenge you, hold you accountable, and help you to grow as Proverbs 27:17 teaches us:

> *As iron sharpens iron,*
> *so one man sharpens another.*

It's extremely important that you don't try to walk in this new relationship with Jesus alone. I encourage you to find a group or at least one person who can help you along the way.

I also challenge you to ask around and do some research to find a Bible-believing,[1] Kingdom-minded[2] church or group of people. Then find someone to teach you how to read the Bible and develop an intimate relationship with God.

Again, ask. Don't worry about feeling awkward. Everyone has been in the same spot as you're in now. In fact, I think you'll find most Christians excited for you and eager to help.

BEGIN TO PRAY ABOUT EVERYTHING. TALK WITH GOD;
HE'S YOUR FRIEND, SO TALK WITH HIM THAT WAY.

Saved From or Saved To?

I want to share another thing I believe we Christians get wrong way too often. More often than not Christians focus too much on the process of salvation as being something that we're being saved from. It's true that once you're saved, you're no longer destined for Hell.

However, I like to look at this as something we're being saved *to*. Not only are we saved *to* an eternal life in Heaven with God but we're also saved so that we can experience life to the full, right here and right now (see John 10:10).

I see very few Christians living "life to the full," and this is perhaps most evident in the way so many men exhibit passive tendencies in their marriages. It's important to understand that our relationship with God through Jesus gives us access to God's power. That power can spur significant changes in our lives and truly help us to live life to the full, including in our roles as husbands and fathers.

Keep the Conversation Going

If you made a decision to follow Jesus while reading this book, would you be willing to let me know by emailing me at info@jimlange.net? It would encourage me so much and allow us to pray for you.

ALSO, IF YOU DO THIS, I'LL SEND YOU A GIFT—
WHICH I BELIEVE WILL HELP YOU GREATLY.

[15]

A FINAL WORD OF ENCOURAGEMENT

During my journey toward freedom and wholeness, there were many times when I thought I was going crazy. Because my thinking was so warped—even though I thought I believed the truth —when I began to walk in truth, it seemed at times I was going off course.

So as we close our time together, I want to encourage you with some words of affirmation.

If any of the stories in this book have resonated with you...

- You're not crazy.
- Though you may be in pain and feel alone, God is for you, He is with you, and He's in your corner.
- God is using this for good in your life (really!).
- You're not alone. I understand your pain. I really do.

Four Seasons of Life

There are four seasons in the life of a Christ-follower:

1. Life is going great; God is there.

2. Life is going great; God does not seem present.
3. Life is not going great or is full of pain; God is there.
4. Life is not going great or is full of pain; God does not seem present (often referred to as the "dark night of the soul").

Because you're reading this book, it's likely you find yourself in either of the last two seasons. I'm so sorry if this is the case, but I have something to share which can encourage you—it's straight from the mouth of your Father in Heaven:

> *"I will give you the treasures of darkness, riches stored in secret places, so that you may know that I am the Lord, the God of Israel, who summons you by name."*
> ~Isaiah 45:3

Let's examine these words briefly:

- God will give you treasures during your dark times.
- He'll reveal riches which are stored in secret places during these times. In other words, you won't discover these unless you're in a dark time.
- It's during dark times that you can know God better.
- He calls you by name during this time.

Having endured some pretty painful situations in my life, I can attest to the truth of this verse. Granted, it didn't always feel this way in the middle of it—but looking back, it's so apparent. If you're in the darkness right now, be encouraged. The Lord promises that He has amazing things to reveal to you!

Wasted Time? Too Late?

Most of us, when faced with the truth of our passivity and timidity, will feel that we've wasted a lot of time leading from passivity and have hurt people—including ourselves—in the process. We may think, "It's too late for me to do anything about it. Besides, God can't use me since I've allowed so much damage."

I could share Scripture after Scripture showing you why the above statements are untrue, but I'll share only three; each from the book of Romans:

> *Therefore, there is now no condemnation for those who are in Christ Jesus, because through Christ Jesus the law of the Spirit of life set me free from the law of sin and death.*
>   *~Romans 8:1–2*

The *therefore* that starts this sentence refers to Jesus dying for our sins and giving us new life in Him (see Romans 6:4 through Romans 8). In other words, because of Jesus' sacrifice, we aren't held guilty of our wrongs. Jesus sets us free.

However, we need to choose to walk free and not keep ourselves in the prison cell to attempt to pay off our own debt. Attempting to do this is prideful and offensive to God. It's saying to Jesus, "What You did isn't enough."

Thank You, Jesus, for allowing us to walk free!

> *For God's gifts and His call are irrevocable. [He never withdraws them when once they are given, and He does not change His mind about those to whom He gives His grace or to whom He sends His call.]*
>   *~Romans 11:29 AMP*

So though we may make a mistake (such as being passive in a marriage), there is *no* condemnation toward us, nor is our calling

162 THE HAPPY WIFE HAPPY LIFE DECEPTION

revoked. In other words, our mess-ups can't remove the calling on our lives.

In the context of what we're discussing, we're each called to be godly men. This is one of the callings He has on our lives. Your passivity and timidity—past or present—doesn't remove that calling —or any other—from you. Hallelujah!

> And we know that in all things God works for the good of those who love
> him, who have been called according to his purpose.
>   ~Romans 8:28

Because this is one of the most quoted verses in the Bible, it's very easy to miss the enormity of its promise. First, we must understand that this promise is for those who love God and are called according to His purpose. If you love God and are a follower of Jesus, God promises that He will use all things—good, bad, painful—for your good.

Did you get that? *All* things. Even the incredible pain and seemingly hopeless situation in your marriage.

"How will all of this affect my kids?" you may ask. *God will work it all out for good.*

"What if I head down this road and things get worse between my wife and me?" *God will work it all out for good.*

"What if I reject passivity and my marriage ends?" *God will work it all out for good.*

He will work *all* things out for the good of those who love Him and are called according to His purpose.

To be clear, this doesn't mean that *all* of these things will be pleasant or pain-free. He doesn't promise that. In fact, Jesus promises the exact opposite in John 16:33 when He says, "In this life you will have trouble."

But, He'll use all of it, even the trouble, for the good of those who love Him and are called according to His purpose.

He's not surprised by your situation. You can release it to Him, He can handle it, and He'll use it for good. It's His promise, and He cannot break a promise (see Romans 8:28, 1 Peter 5:7, Revelation 22:13).

When you're in the midst of this pain, remember that it's critical to be on the lookout for shame because it's so easy to let it take over.

WHEN WE THINK ABOUT OUR PAST MISTAKES AND BELIEVE THINGS CONTRARY TO THE THREE VERSES ABOVE, WE COME CLOSE TO BECOMING BEST FRIENDS WITH SHAME. SHAME IS NOT FROM GOD, BUT RATHER IT IS A FAVORITE TOOL OF OUR ENEMY.

Meditate regularly on these three verses from Romans above. Make them your best friend, walk in the truth, and combat shame.

Friend or Foe?

Should you decide to stand up and reject passivity, I'd be remiss if I didn't tell you that not everyone will approve of what you're doing. We already discussed how your wife will likely oppose it, at least at first. However, some unlikely people in your life also may not be on board with your new plan.

It's possible that your children may be less than pleased with you. Remember—leaving your comfort zone causes those close to you to have to exit theirs as well.

Even some pastors, leaders in your church, and other Christians may try to convince you that you're not following God. Some people —including church leaders—are so steeped in religion that they can't see the truth. This isn't their fault. Truthfully, they simply haven't been educated about this line of thinking yet.

Satan is known as the "accuser of the brethren" (see Revelation 12:10). He often uses other people to make accusations against us. The difficult part of this is that he's very crafty, and it can ignite great doubt in us.

This can strengthen the voice of our inner critic—the person inside who whispers about how we're wrong, not good enough, not deserving, not righteous, etc. This voice—as well as the others mentioned here—is often loud and convincing.

So how do you know which voice is truth and which voice is "the accuser?"

It's critical that you seek wise counsel, as we've discussed. However, if you listen to everyone, you can become confused. This is why building a Life-Team will be critical for you (see Chapter 9).

When people give you conflicting information, it's important to take it to your Life-Team to seek their counsel and ask them to speak truth to you. I cannot emphasize this point strongly enough: find a Life Team (and if you need help with this, see Chapter 16).

Jesus dealt with naysayers too, and they were primarily church leaders. When faced with negative input (which can sound so convincing), realize that it's not your job to convince them.

Instead respond with something like, "Thank you so much for sharing that with me. I'll give that consideration." Debating with them will rarely prove fruitful (although it can be at times—you'll need to discern when it's appropriate).

Marriage and Divorce Revisited

The Bible is clear: God hates divorce (and other things listed in Proverbs 6:16–19—many of which can lead to divorce). I, too, hate divorce. But I also hate the religious bondage that shackles many men in the body of Christ.

I am for marriage, and my prayer for you is that your marriage is restored. I am also for you, and I hate abuse of all kinds, especially in marriage. And today it seems that the abuse of men in marriage is not discussed. This has to change.

I do know this: the path to a healthy marriage begins when you stand up and become healthy. However, even if you do this, it's possible that restoration of your relationship still won't happen.

A question that I've asked myself often is one I'm now going to ask you:

CAN YOU CONTINUE ON YOUR CURRENT PATH OF PASSIVITY AND TIMIDITY AND STILL HONOR GOD?

I encourage you to ponder this question and process it with your Life-Team.

Jesus came to set the captives free (see Luke 4:18). It's time for you to walk free from the bondage of fear.

Not Only About You

Earlier we learned that the courageous journey you're embarking on is more than just about you, but it's also about helping to change the course of generations of marriages and relationships in your family for years to come. However, you're a part of something even bigger than that.

As we discussed in Chapter 3 and Chapter 4, manhood has been under attack. This has contributed to the passivity epidemic we see in men throughout the world. This doesn't honor God in any way, and it does not honor women. In fact, it actually hurts them.

God put His plan for husband and wife in place to benefit each of us. Unfortunately, this plan has been skewed. So now it's time we turned the tide and regained what has been lost—not for our selfish reasons but to honor God and to help rescue others.

Jesus quotes the first few verses of Isaiah 61 in Luke 4:18–19. However, I believe the entire chapter is for us—men emerging from passivity into assertiveness. I encourage you to read it and see if you agree.

The following is a summary from each of the 11 verses in Isaiah 61 and what I believe this means to you and me:

- V. 1 Through this book you're reading, I'm proclaiming freedom and release from darkness for you.
- V. 2 I'm proclaiming God's favor and vengeance on your behalf and that He would comfort you in your mourning.
- V. 3 My purpose is to help you to turn your mourning and depression into joy and praise and to help you become oaks of righteousness... strong in the Lord.
- V. 4 You will then rebuild what the enemy has destroyed. You will help start a tidal wave of hope for men (and, as a result, families)... a men's movement.
- V. 5 God will turn the hearts of those once against us so much that they will do some of our work.
- V. 6 We shall be known as ministers of God. We will also eat the wealth of the nations, and we will possess the glory our captors once had.
- V. 7 Instead of shame, we will receive double of what we've lost, including joy.
- V. 8 God loves justice and hates wrong, especially when cloaked in religion, and He will faithfully repay us and make an everlasting covenant with us.
- V. 9 You will be prosperous and blessed as will your offspring.
- V. 10 God has clothed us in robes of righteousness.
- V. 11 The Lord will bring forth rightness, justice, and praise in our lives.

I encourage you to teach other men what you're learning. Are there other men you could help? Perhaps you know men who need to read this book. Sending a quick email with a link to the book might be a small gesture that could change someone's life

Parting the Water

I would like to close our time together by looking at two places in Scripture in which the Lord split bodies of water to allow people to walk through. The first is the most famous account: Moses' parting of the Red Sea (see Exodus 14:15–22). In the second, the Lord parted the Jordan River so the Israelites could enter the Promised Land (see Joshua 3).

In both cases, God's power parted—or split—bodies of water so that the Israelites could walk through on dry land. However, that's where the similarities end.

The Wilderness

In the case of the Red Sea crossing, the Israelites needed to cross to keep from being captured or killed by Pharaoh's army. Moses obeyed God and simply raised his staff, the sea parted, and the Israelites were saved.

God wanted to take them into their destiny (the Promised Land) but because of their poor choices after escaping Egypt, they remained in the desert for 40 years. They were supposed to go *through* the wilderness but instead got stuck *in* the wilderness.

You may be reading this because you're feeling stuck in the "wilderness" in your marriage. God has different intentions for you— He has a better way. He wants to take you from your desert… into your Promised Land.

The Promised Land

Now for the other story about parting water. After 40 years, and after the death of Moses, God asked Joshua to lead the Israelites into their destiny, the Promised Land. In order to enter, however, they needed to cross the Jordan River, while it was at flood stage.

God told the four high priests—who carried the Ark of the

Covenant on poles—to take the ark and stand in the river, *and then* He would part the river.

Think about the ramifications of this. When a river is at flood stage, several things change:

1. The river's current flows much stronger and moves much faster.
2. The river picks up dirt and sediment from the riverbank, making the river muddy.
3. The muddy water hides what lies below the river's bank, making footing treacherous.

Now imagine being one of the four priests who carried the ark on poles. Let's say you're one of the two in front. You must take that first step into the fast-running, muddy water.

You might be thinking, "What if I slip and drop the Ark of the Covenant?" or "What if I slip and am swept away by the current?" or "What if I stumble and touch the ark (which would cause immediate death – see 2 Samuel 6:7)?"

None of these are pleasant options. Yet God asked them to do it anyway.

It seems to me that it would've been much easier on the priests had God simply said, "Stand on the bank of the river, and I will separate the water for you." Yet He didn't. Why?

GOD WANTED OBEDIENCE AND FAITH FROM THE ISRAELITES IN ORDER FOR THEM TO BEGIN TO TAKE POSSESSION OF THEIR INHERITANCE.

He wanted them to exhibit faith and "step out" into the water without knowing what the outcome might be.

But that's not all. In addition to obedience, God needed the Israelites to be courageous. The reason? Because *after* the Israelites entered the Promised Land, they needed to fight many battles in order to take possession of their land.

He asks the same of you (and me) in this very moment. To enter your Promised Land and claim your inheritance will require tremendous obedience, courage, and faith. It will require you to step out into some uncharted and fast-moving waters without knowing what the future holds. And you—more than likely—will face some battles.

Entering your Promised Land will require you to be obedient and courageous with the full understanding that it could be difficult and painful.

But know that your obedience and courage pleases God greatly because you're trusting Him at new levels. And remember: though it may be difficult at times, the Promised Land is better than where you are today.

The Promised Land is a place of healing and freedom for you. This is about trusting God and not trying to control the outcomes in your marriage or in any other area of your life.

A man of obedience, courage and faith will continue to move toward his Promised Land knowing that this is his best chance for a healthy, godly marriage.

IT TAKES GREAT COURAGE FOR A MAN WHO HAS BEEN BEATEN DOWN REPEATEDLY BY HIS WIFE TO DECLARE, "NO MORE."

IT TAKES GREAT COURAGE FOR A MAN WHO IS AFRAID OF LOSING OUT ON SEX[1] TO LOVINGLY ENTER THE "DANGER ZONE" AND CONFRONT HIS WIFE.

IT TAKES GREAT COURAGE FOR A MAN TO REACH OUT AND ASK WISE OTHERS FOR HELP OR TO BE ON HIS LIFE-TEAM.

IT TAKES GREAT COURAGE FOR A MAN WHO HAS BEEN TRAPPED
BY FEAR TO FINALLY SAY, "HONEY, WE NEED TO TALK."

Mighty warrior, I have confidence in you.
You can do this. Your time is now!

*"Be strong and courageous. Do not be terrified; do not be discouraged, for the
Lord your God will be with you wherever you go."*

~Joshua 1:9b

[16]

YOU'RE NOT ALONE

While I was learning to break free from passivity, I assembled a Life-Team. They were incredibly helpful. I never could have done it on my own, and I'm *so* thankful for them!

They continually spoke truth to me and encouraged me. And they helped me to feel loved and not so alone.

As mentioned earlier, I have not met a man who has broken free from the grips of passivity and timidity without the guidance of wise others. A Life-Team composed of the right kind of people is critical for you in your journey. Get this wrong and you could be further deceived.

Many men struggle to assemble such a team. Below are some tips that can help you.

What to look for

One of the primary reasons that assembling a Life-Team can be difficult is that most of us want to be agreed with so we naturally gather people around us who believe as we do. After all, who loves to be told they're wrong?

But having people in your life willing to speak truth, even when it's difficult to hear, will help you immensely in your journey to break free from passivity and timidity.

In my work with passive and timid men, I've noticed that many of us have been deceived and don't realize that we believe lies. Furthermore, we can so easily get caught focusing on the behavior of our wives rather on ourselves.

In order to break free from these lies and to stay focused on the only person we can change—us—we need others to boldly speak the truth to us, and do so continually—even if it's uncomfortable for them and us. Proverbs 27:6 says, "Wounds from a friend can be trusted, but an enemy multiplies kisses."

It is also good to find some people who have experience in helping people with relationship issues. Pastors, counselors, coaches or those who lead a marriage ministry work well. You may need to pay some of these people for their guidance, especially if this is how they earn a living. This is an investment in yourself... and you're worth it.

Another thing that is paramount is that these people need to show that they're for you. If you sense any jealousy in them, ask someone else.

A bonus would be to find a man or two who has successfully found freedom from passivity and timidity. This isn't always easy, but they're out there. If you can't find anyone like this, see below (*A Guy Who Made a Huge Difference*) for a suggestion that can help you.

To summarize, here are the recommended characteristics for your Life-Team members[1] (including some additional traits):

- They are willing to tell you the truth, even when it's uncomfortable
- They have experience in helping people with relationship issues
- They are for you and not jealous of you in any way; they are willing to make time for you
- They are trustworthy; they will keep everything said confidential

- They are at least as far along as you in their faith
- They exhibit wisdom in their life
- They have a heart to help others
- They are safe; you feel comfortable sharing with them

As mentioned, it would also be tremendously helpful that one or two members of your Life-Team have personal experience in breaking free from passivity and timidity. Let's take a look at why this is so important.

A Guy Who Made a Huge Difference

If you study the life of Jesus in the four gospels (Matthew, Mark, Luke and John) you see that he walked closely with His 12 disciples. You might call them His Life-Team.

Scripture also suggests that He had a more intimate relationship with three of those: Peter, James and John (see Matthew 17:1, 26:36-37, Mark 10:35).

And, it appears He had an even closer relationship with John (see John 19:26-27).

12 – 3 – 1: a good model for us to consider when assembling our Life-Team. An effective team might have a larger number of people you consult with regularly (but not necessarily as a group), a smaller number you talk with more frequently, and one person who acts as your mentor, or closest confidante.

One of the members of my team was very skilled at helping others trapped in passivity and timidity. He had also been through the battle of passivity in his own marriage, and he had the scars to prove it. But he had conquered it, and I cannot tell you how helpful he was to me as he shared the things he learned, the things that worked, and the things that didn't work.

Unfortunately, I didn't meet him until much later in my journey. Though I'm extremely grateful for the role he played in my life and though it has been worth much more than the money I spent with him (I had hired him as my coach), had I recruited him to my team earlier, it would have kept me from a lot of pain.

If a trusted person in your life has broken free from his passivity, that's great—ask him to be a member of your Life-Team. If not, let's talk.

Because of the path I've walked, I have a passion for helping men break free from passivity and timidity and helping them become the men God has called them to be. I've been privileged to guide many men through their struggles, accelerate their growth, and help them find true freedom. It would be an honor to speak with you and possibly walk with you on your journey.

Here are the two best ways to get ahold of me:

1. Email me at coaching@jimlange.net; or
2. Visit https://jimlange.net/coach/ and I, or someone on my team, will be in touch to schedule a conversation.

As I say goodbye, I want to thank you for the privilege of sharing my heart with you. It shows that you're serious about finding freedom. I'm proud of you. I know God has great things in store for you.

If you'd like some additional resources, I hope you enjoy the gift I'm offering you on the next page.

Blessings to you!
- Jim

FREE BONUSES WITH YOUR BOOK

There is hope... Regain respect—and intimacy—in your marriage.

https://jimlange.net/bonus

A **FREE** Membership Website for Men
to Radically Grow Yourself and Revolutionize Your Marriage.

You'd be shocked at how many husbands have experienced disrespect, manipulation, and rejection in their marriages. Difficulties with your wife can leave you feeling like a failure, hopeless, and worn out.

I know; I've been there. God wants peace and rest in your home.

LEARN TO NAVIGATE
Navigate relationships with people who
control, manipulate, and reject you.

REGAIN HOPE.
Get unstuck and experience hope again.

RECONNECT.
Reconnect to your spouse emotionally,
relationally, and sexually.

You don't have to be stuck in a painful marriage for the rest of your life. Get access to your FREE Resources on the *Happy Wife Happy Life Deception* Bonus Site!

Get your free resources here...

https://jimlange.net/bonus

Jim grew up in NW Ohio, and after four years playing basketball and majoring in computer systems at the University of Toledo, he began his career as a programmer.

As his skillset expanded, he moved into computer consulting then transitioned into hardware and software sales. Jim's sales experience grew to include commercial insurance and healthcare, and he ended his sales career as a Vice President before starting his own business.

Jim has worked in the business arena for over 30 years where he has honed his leadership skills.

Thanks to his many diverse leadership roles in business, the Church, and his community, Jim has led over 200 leaders in monthly executive roundtable groups.

In 2004, Jim started his own business with a focus on developing Christians in areas such as business, leadership, relationships, marriage, emotional issues, and finding overall success in life.

As a sought-after adviser and coach, Jim knows how to ask the right questions. He helps people solve their biggest problems through life-coaching, public speaking, authoring, and consulting. In all he does, he brings experience, problem-solving skills, and passion to help others.

Jim is a #1 best-selling and award-winning author having written such works as *Bleedership: Biblical First-Aid for Leaders* and *Calming the Storm Within: How to Find Peace in this Chaotic World* as well as three other books.

He resides in NW Ohio and is the father to three grown children and a grandpa to two.

Some recommendations on Jim's LinkedIn profile:

"If you need an excellent coach with keen business insights and a heart of gold, call Jim Lange! Jim works hard to help leaders find what they need to grow their impact and success. He helps people get unstuck and get connected to the people and the resources they need. Jim has a huge heart for Christ

and his mission is to help us bring Christ more fully into our lives and our work." Don't wait to talk with Jim- you'll be so blessed when you do!

I have had regular interaction with Jim since 2009, his sincerity, dedication, & commitment to helping others is refreshing, insightful and needed in today's business culture. If you're looking for someone to give you valuable insight and discernment then I encourage to connect with Jim.

Jim is a man on a mission...to equip, encourage, and empower leaders to be successful in the marketplace and at home. He is a man of integrity and excellence devoted to serving others, helping them achieve their God-given potential...body, mind, and soul. I am grateful for his involvement in my life and highly recommend him.

Jim has been a tremendous encouragement to me along the journey to find meaning and purpose in life. With much of his own personal story captured in his book, Calming the Storm Within: How to Find Peace in This Chaotic World, *Jim is able to relate firsthand to one's desire to truly experience "peace" in this life. I highly recommend using Jim as a resource to come alongside you as a "guide" whether that be through his books, executive round-tables, one-on-one coaching, or various other resources Jim has to offer. Jim's become a friend and one of my top key advisors in the journey and I hope that can be the same for you.*

Jim is one of the finest men I have ever known. Not only is he one of my closest friends, but he is an incredibly effective leader and communicator. He leads and lives with character, integrity, and genuine humility. He is a highly accomplished author and business leader, and offers a very unique blend of practical experience with compelling vision to help business and marketplace leaders become who and what they were to created to be. If the opportunity to work with Jim presents itself, I can't think of a better person than he that you could work with.

I not only look up to Jim because of his height but more importantly, I look up to Jim because of his courage, his convictions and his gift of speaking truth! His faith has strengthened mine and I am a better man because of his influence and leadership. Jim reminds us all that we cannot be different people in the different roles we have in life. We are the same person in our profession that we are at home and in the community. He challenges us, through his daily example, to keep our priorities in order and build on a solid foundation of a closer relationship with our creator. Literally, "Thank God" for blessing my life with Jim Lange! I know I am not alone in that prayer.

FIND JIM ON SOCIAL MEDIA!

LinkedIn: JimLange.net/linkedin
Facebook: JimLange.net/facebook
Twitter: JimLange.net/twitter
YouTube: JimLange.net/youtube

Hire Jim to Speak

If you host events for men (or know someone who does), I'd love to speak with you. One of my passions is speaking, and I'd love to present a meaningful and fun message that can make a huge impact on your group.

If you'd like to bring a unique, engaging, and life-changing experience that can radically impact men's lives, please contact me. I would be honored to discuss your event with you.

Email speaking@jimlange.net to begin the conversation.

Hire Jim as Your Coach

I have never met a man who has broken free from passivity and timidity on his own. In my case, I had about a dozen people on my Life-Team who played key roles in me finding freedom. There's no way I could have done it alone.

One man on my team helped me greatly because he was an expert coach adept at navigating passivity, timidity, and the complexity of marital relationships. Also, he had experienced similar things in his marriage before he found freedom.

He fully understood my situation since he had been there himself. I paid him very well, and his input proved invaluable. This was the single greatest investment I've made in my life.

I only wish I had engaged with him earlier. Had I done so, my time of pain would've been shortened significantly.

I'm passionate about helping men break free from the chains of passivity and timidity, and live a life they never imagined. If you don't have someone like this in your life, let's talk. I'd be honored to speak with you.

If you're interested in engaging in coaching with me, shoot me an email at coaching@jimlange.net.

Can I Ask A Favor?

Would you consider leaving me a candid (but positive) review on Amazon for this book? Reviews mean a lot to me, and it will greatly help me to spread this message of hope to men around the world. I would be very grateful if you would do so.

If you decide to do that, be sure to let me know at info@jimlange.net so I can say thanks.

QUICK! WHO WAS THE WORST BOSS YOU EVER HAD?

Chances are, you'll recognize him/her in the pages of Jim Lange's bestselling book, *Bleedership, Biblical First Aid for Leaders*—a book that combines biblical principles with leadership skills.

Wounds, cuts, and bruises abound wherever you find uninspired employees, a fearful staff, or a company or organization in disarray from the top down. *Bleedership* delivers the cure when leadership falls short.

This fast-paced, page-turning book demonstrates the profound difference a godly, sound leader can make in a business, a church, or a home. It's all here— great quotes from some of our greatest leaders; true-life stories; scenarios offered to bring the reader to make a decision as to who was the good leader or bad leader in each situation.

Full of biblical references, refreshing insight, and wise, common-sense solutions, *Bleedership* is the book you'll want to pick up for yourself and then grab an extra to pass to a leader or a potential leader you know today!

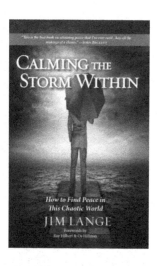

ONE OF THE FEW CONSTANTS IN LIFE IS CHANGE.

Our lives are so unpredictable. Jobs are lost. Health falters. Loved ones pass away. Relationships get rocky. Stress comes like a tidal wave.

Being a follower of Jesus doesn't necessarily make it easier. In fact, He told us we'd have trouble in this life: In this world you will have trouble...That means all of us. Guaranteed.

While Jesus didn't leave us without hope, trouble often brings with it a lack of peace. We become prisoners to worry, anxiety and fear. Thankfully, Jesus didn't stop there. We CAN be free.

After making this prediction of trouble in our lives, Jesus was also quick to remind us that He is bigger than any of our troubles: But take heart! I have overcome the world.

Jesus not only came to provide a way to Heaven—He came to give us life to the full. That means inner peace in recessions. Serenity in the midst of relationship struggles. Calm regardless of circumstances.

This isn't just any kind of peace...it is the peace which transcends all understanding, a level of peace that we cannot imagine. And God has made this readily available.

So take hold of this peace. It's meant for you.

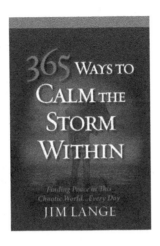

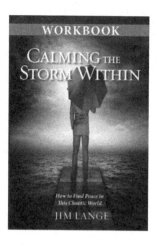

THE PEACE THAT SURPASSES ALL UNDERSTANDING IS WITHIN YOUR GRASP!

Jim Lange invites you to join him in the quest for true and authentic peace which can be found with God's help.

On your own or in a group, journey through the 15 sessions of this workbook and discover key principles that will make peace a reality in your life, including:

- Where peace comes from and why it is available to you;
- Why embracing chaos in your life is advantageous;
- The truth about peace stealers;
- The path to peace;
- The #1 key to finding peace;
- The role of intimacy in living a life filled with peace;
- How obedience determines your level of peace;
- Where you can find the most help in your quest for peace;
- How joy and gentleness can impact peace;
- Why prayer is so important;
- Why your focus can determine how peaceful you are;
- The role that planning can play in your search for peace;
- ...and how to practically implement peace in your daily life.

ACKNOWLEDGEMENTS

I spent a great deal of time in this book developing the concept of Life-Team. Community is critical. In much the same way, I had an amazing team who helped to guide me, challenge me, and encourage me during the writing of this book.

I'm not sure this could have happened without the support and prayers of my Intercessory Team. Thank you Bonnie, Rod, Theresa, Jane, Caryn and Scott. I appreciate you more than you know.

Thank you to the many others who read this manuscript at different stages, encouraged me, offered incredibly valuable feedback, and would often speak truth to me even when it was sometimes painful:

Missy Anders, Rod Brant, Conrad and Peggy Beck, John Beckett, Chris and Kristin Bonham, Marquetta Breslin, Dave Crabill, Brenton Dearing, Theresa DeWitt, Scott Estep, Greg Hackett, Carolyn Hapka, Charles Hollensed, Robert Hotchkin, James Johnson, Cheryl Kinnersley, Jeff Kistler, Sharon Lange, Mary Michel, Kevin Miller, Mark Miller, Melvin Pillay, Chuck Proudfit, Doug Reiter, Vince Rocha, Dana Schaefer, Greg Schlueter, Kirk Schneemann, Michelle Seidler, Ben Snyder, Bob Tamasy, Ford Taylor, Kevin VanErt and Kathy White.

Ben Wolf, thank you for your excellent and thorough job of editing this work. Your efforts helped to make this book significantly better. I am so thankful for you.

There are five others to whom I'd like to give special honor:

Glenn Pearson, thank you for the countless hours you spent going through my manuscript and reviewing your suggestions with me in numerous phone conversations. Your input was very helpful.

Rich Marshall, thank you for your pastor's heart and your

sensitive challenge which led to an entire chapter being added. I am so thankful for you.

Perry Marshall, you went above and beyond. Not only did you introduce me to Ben, my editor, but you gave me extremely thoughtful counsel as to how I could make this book more powerful. Thank you Perry, I appreciate you.

Scott David, this project could not have happened without your ongoing support, counsel and brainstorming. I cannot even estimate the hours we spent together going through pieces of the manuscript and arguing our views until we came to agreement. You are a special friend and I thank the Lord for you!

Finally, Lord, I thank You for Your immense goodness and for the incredible amount of grace and love You have showered upon me. You are so good. And thank You also for allowing intense hardship into my life, without which this project would not have happened. I love you Papa!

APPENDIX: A Word For Wives

If you're a wife who's reading this, you're probably doing so for one of three reasons. One, you can't believe someone would write a book to help men who struggle with passivity and timidity. *After all, hasn't it been men who've abused women since the beginning of time?*

Two, you discovered that your husband is reading this book, and you're wondering why he would do so. This may even hurt and anger you.

Three, you feel that your husband is controlling and that you've been the passive one, and you're wondering why this isn't written for women as well as men.

I want to address each of these.

First, I agree that the behaviors of some men over time—and even presently—are abhorrent. This book is not written for them.

My hope and prayer is that this book helps a unique group of men who are the polar opposites of abusive husbands. Though you may not know men like this, I assure you they are everywhere.

Second, I can't tell you for sure why your husband is reading this. But based on my work with men in the context of their marriages, I can share with you why I believe he bought this book.

Your husband is reading this because of his love for you. I know that may surprise you, but it's true. He wants to be the man God made him to be. He wants to fight for your marriage and make it the best marriage possible.

He isn't giving up. Instead he's recognizing that his job is not to change you; he's the only one he can change. He wants to grow to become a godly husband, and he has recognized that his passivity is not God's design.

My reason for writing this book is to help men learn from the mistakes I—and others—have made. I've heard it said that a smart man learns from his own mistakes, and a wise man learns from the mistakes of others. Your husband is a wise man and is attempting to learn from our mistakes.

Would you consider praying for him and encouraging him in this? I know he would appreciate it, and I believe it would help your marriage.

Third, if you feel that you're the passive one and your husband is controlling then I'm so sorry you're in an abusive marriage. I truly am. Though this book is written for men, I'm confident that you, too, can find keys in its pages that will help you to break free from the prison of passivity.

ENDNOTES

1. GETTING PERSONAL

1. *While this book is written primarily in the context of a marital relationship, the principles shared are applicable to any relationship.*
2. *For a list of suggested resources, go to jimlange.net/Bonus*
3. *Robert Lewis, Men's Fraternity: The Quest For Authentic Manhood (Nashville, TN Lifeway Press).*

3. THE EPIDEMIC OF PASSIVITY: EXTERNAL CONTRIBUTORS

1. *http://foundations.uwgb.org/family/*
2. *Evid Based Complement Alternat Med. 2005 Dec; 2(4): 503–512. doi: 10.1093/ecam/neh127 PMCID: PMC1297500 PMID: 16322808 Post-Traumatic Stress Disorder: Evidence-Based Research for the Third Millennium.*
3. *Kulka RA, Schlenger WE, Fairbank JA, Hough RL, Jordan CB, Marmar CR, et al. Trauma and the Vietnam war generation: Report of findings from the National Veterans Readjustment Study. NY: Brunner/Mazel; 1990*
4. *For an article about the affect of this on young men, see: http://theconversation.com/act-tough-and-hide-weakness-research-reveals-pressure-young-men-are-under-74898*
5. *Walter L. Liefeld, Ephesians, vol. 10, The IVP New Testament Commentary Series (Downers Grove, IL: InterVarsity Press, 1997), Eph 5:22.*

4. THE EPIDEMIC OF PASSIVITY: OTHER FACTORS

1. *Jordan B. Peterson, 12 Rules for Life (Toronto, Ontario Canada, Random House Canada), 59-60.*
2. *I am deeply grateful to Robert Lewis for introducing this to me through* Men's Fraternity, The Quest For Authentic Manhood.
3. *In some cases, a wife's behavior may be symptomatic of an underlying physical or mental issue that only a qualified physician or mental health professional can properly diagnose.*

5. THE EPIDEMIC OF PASSIVITY: INTERNAL CONTRIBUTORS

1. *For strategies on how to navigate the lack of physical intimacy in your marriage, go to https://jimlange.net/bonus*
2. *Oxford Dictionary of English (Oxford University Press, USA; 3rd Revised Edition)*

8. DISENGAGE

1. *James Strong, Enhanced Strong's Lexicon (Woodside Bible Fellowship, 1995).*
2. *Francis Frangipane, The Three Battlegrounds (Cedar Rapids, IA Advancing Church Publications), 117.*

9. YOUR LIFE-TEAM

1. http://www.rewildchurch.com/2016/09/18/division-the-spirit-of-diabolos/

10. HEALING & LOVING CONFRONTATION

1. *https://biblehub.com/hebrew/7853.htm; https://biblehub.com/hebrew/7854.htm*
2. *For strategies on how to navigate the lack of physical intimacy in your marriage, go to https://jimlange.net/bonus.*
3. *To read the full letter, go to jimlange.net/Bonus*

12. FREEDOM BLUEPRINT

1. *For some tips on journaling go to jimlange.net/Bonus*
2. *For a helpful Life-Team Building Tool go to https://jimlange.net/bonus*

13. BREAKING THE CYCLE

1. *Robert Lewis, Men's Fraternity: The Quest For Authentic Manhood (Nashville, TN Lifeway Press).*
2. I'm indebted to Robert Lewis and his teachings about the power of ceremony in *Raising the Modern Day Knight.*
3. *For a 6-step apology process go to jimlange.net/Bonus*

14. THE ONLY WAY

1. *By "Bible-believing" I am referring to people who not only read the scriptures regularly, but believe God's word is true, and make efforts to live their life by what they learn in the bible.*
2. *By "Kingdom-minded" I am referring to people who strive to put God's Kingdom first in their life. They are focused on the King and doing His will.*

15. A FINAL WORD OF ENCOURAGEMENT

1. *For strategies on how to navigate the lack of physical intimacy in your marriage, go to https://jimlange.net/bonus.*

16. YOU'RE NOT ALONE

1. *For a helpful Life-Team Building Tool go to https://jimlange.net/bonus*

ABOUT THE AUTHOR

1. *Special thank you to Scott David and Scott Estep for writing this section.*

Made in USA - North Chelmsford, MA
133797U_9780988613775
10.27.2022 1603